Twitter for Authors

A BUSY WRITER'S GUIDE

Marcy Kennedy

Tongue Untied Communications
ONTARIO, CANADA

Marcy Kennedy
marcykennedy@gmail.com
www.marcykennedy.com

Book Layout ©2013 BookDesignTemplates.com
Edited by Chris J. Saylor
Cover Design by Melinda VanLone

Twitter for Authors/ Marcy Kennedy —1st ed.
ISBN 978-0-9920371-9-2

Contents

Seven Reasons Why Every Writer Needs to Be on Twitter

Twitter often gets a bad reputation from people who don't understand it, misunderstand it as full of spam and celebrity stalkers, or don't know how to use it to its full potential to build an author platform.

When used correctly, though, Twitter can be one of the best tools for meeting new readers and increasing traffic to your blog. And it's fun!

Don't believe me? Well, let me prove it to you. I have seven reasons why I think every writer should be using Twitter.

Reason #1: Twitter has over 100 million active accounts, and is still growing.

Whether you're seeking traditional publication or plan to self-publish, whether you're a non-fiction author, a novelist, a poet, or a short-story writer, you need a platform to sell your work. Your readers are on Twitter. You just need to know how to meet them.

This is true even if you write children's books or YA. If you write for kids, your readers might not be on Twitter, but their parents and aunts and uncles and even grandparents are, and your books might just be the perfect gift they're looking for.

Reason #2: Twitter allows you to build a following faster than any other social networking site.

People who find you on Facebook usually already know you or know about you. People who find you on Twitter are more likely to be complete strangers (at first) because of the ability to participate in conversations through hashtags.

Reason #3: Twitter makes you a better writer.

Twitter gives you 140 characters to work with. Not 140 letters or 140 words, but 140 characters. Spaces count, and so do punctuation and URLs (links).

Working within those constraints forces you to write tighter. No purple prose allowed. No weak verbs modified by adjectives. You need to figure out exactly what you're trying to say. Those skills translate directly into better writing elsewhere.

Reason #4: Twitter brings you the news faster than any news site can.

Twitter is real-time, which means that, while reporters are putting together their stories and getting approval from their editors, normal people on site are tweeting. In August 2011, Twitter lit up like a firefly on crack about the magnitude 5.8 earthquake in Virginia—before the news stations could catch their balance. My husband called my mother-in-law right away to make sure she and the rest of the family there were safe.

In the plague of tornadoes that rolled through Texas in April 2012, Twitter might have even saved lives. (If you'd like to read the post about this, search for "Twitter & Twisters—A Life-Saving Combination" by Kristen Lamb.) So many tornadoes hit the Dallas area at once that meteorologists couldn't keep up, even if people still had electricity and the ability to check their televisions, use their computers, or tune in on the radio. But what everyone could still do was tweet using their phones. People banded together to warn others and report sightings, keeping all involved safer than they could have been alone.

Reason #5: Twitter allows you to keep your finger on the pulse of the publishing industry.

Twitter is like a writer's Mecca because you can quickly find out about interesting and informative new blog posts (already vetted by others); keep up on industry trends and new releases; and get tips on writing and publishing from agents, editors, and best-selling authors. No searching involved. It comes to you in a bite-sized 140-character nugget. If you decide you want more, you click the link.

Reason #6: Twitter helps you research.

In her bestselling book *We Are Not Alone: A Writer's Guide to Social Media*, Kristen Lamb tells the story of how she needed information on bounty hunters for her novel. Rather than wasting hours trying to sort through results on Google and still not coming up with what she needed, she tweeted about it and received replies from actual bounty hunters willing to answer her questions.

But it's not only facts you can research on Twitter. If you're not sure your main character's name is a good fit for their personality and job, ask. If you want to know what writing software other writers actually trust, ask. (I did, and fell in love with Scrivener.)

In my co-written novel, we mentioned Sodom and Gomorrah, and we debated whether enough people would know what we meant. So I asked, and we ended up leaving it in the book.

Reason #7: Twitter gives you a support network of friends.

I've left this for last because, to me, it's the most important. Writing is solitary. We sit at our computers and play with our imaginary friends. Which is great, but also leaves us without the support network we need if we want to make writing a long-term career.

On Twitter, you'll find someone to talk you down off the ledge when one too many rejections or poor reviews leave you wanting to quit writing altogether. On Twitter, you can make writer friends who'll run word sprints with you to help you keep on track. On Twitter, you can make reader friends who'll be excited to go out and buy your book and tell everyone about it.

HOW IS TWITTER DIFFERENT FROM FACEBOOK AND OTHER SOCIAL MEDIA SITES?

I've hopefully convinced you of the value of Twitter, but you might still be wondering how Twitter is different from all the other social media sites people are telling you about.

Let me quickly walk you through the major sites, how they're different in tone and focus, and why I love Twitter the best.

LinkedIn is like a professional networking event. You go there to get references and endorsements, pass around your resume, and keep your tie straight. Personal and professional boundaries are firm.

Facebook is like a backyard BBQ. People come for an hour or two. They sit. They chat. They swap baby photos. People expect you to be there.

Google+ is like a convention—techies, nerds, geeks, graphic designers, photographers, gamers, college students, and writers. In the same way that conventions are about people connecting over a shared passion, so is Google+. What works on other social media sites doesn't necessarily work here.

Pinterest is the salon. You swap recipes and fashion and beauty tips. It's pretty and soothing and very visual.

Twitter is the workplace water cooler, which is why, in my opinion, it's one of the most valuable social media sites. You can talk work. You can talk news. You can just chat about your weekend. You don't need to be there for large chunks of time. You stop by a couple times a day, chat with new people each time, and go back to work.

What more could you ask for?

HOW THIS BOOK IS SET UP

I've designed this book so that you'll benefit from it no matter your experience level with Twitter.

If you're brand-new to Twitter and don't even have an account, just start at Part One, where I walk you through setting up your account, and keep going at your own pace. This book will work best if you apply the contents of each chapter before moving on to the next. I've packed this book full of information, which means you'll probably feel overwhelmed if you try to read it straight through from cover to cover. It isn't meant to be read from cover to cover in one sitting. It's meant to be worked through as a practical guide, with Twitter open in front of you.

If you have some experience with Twitter, this book will help you improve your knowledge of what Twitter has to offer and help you use it more effectively. I still recommend that you start at the beginning and at least skim the set-up chapters to make sure your foundation is solid before moving on, but you'll find the freshest information in Parts Two and Three.

Here's what you'll find in the rest of the book.

PART ONE: Getting Started

Chapter One: A Philosophy of Social Media

Chapter Two: Getting Signed Up and Set Up on Twitter

Chapter Three: How to Set Your Notifications

Chapter Four: How to Design Your Twitter Page

Chapter Five: Essential Terminology

Chapter Six: How to Write Your Twitter Bio

Chapter Seven: TweetDeck vs. Hootsuite

PART TWO: Continuing Strong

Chapter Eight: How to Stay Safe on Twitter

Chapter Nine: Building Columns and Using Them to Find Readers

Chapter Ten: Creating and Using Lists

Chapter Eleven: Link Shorteners

Chapter Twelve: Hashtags

Chapter Thirteen: What Should We Tweet About?

Chapter Fourteen: Writing Tweets that Get Clicked and Shared

Chapter Fifteen: Scheduling and Automation: Evil or Helpful?

Chapter Sixteen: Time Management on Twitter

PART THREE: Advanced Techniques

BEFORE WE GET STARTED…

I know that, as soon as you have a Twitter account, it's going to be tempting to start following every big name in your industry. ***Don't.***

As much as I hate to say it, a big part of Twitter is the social proof of numbers. If you jump in and follow everyone and their neighbor, when those people get their notifications, they're going to see that you're following 100 people (or more) but only have two people following you.

Do you know what happens to people like that? They get deleted. They don't get the follow-backs they're hoping for. Because everyone is suspicious about why no one wants to follow them.

I'll take you to the point where you can follow the bigger names without worrying about whether they follow you back or not, but there's an order to things. So, once you get your account made, just sit tight. I'll let you know when you're ready to start tweeting and following.

If you're already on Twitter, keep doing what you've been doing and change what you need to as we work through the process.

WHO AM I?

Many people want to know the credentials of the writer of a book before they buy it. If you're one of those people, this section is for you. Why am I qualified to teach writers about Twitter?

I'm not a social media expert. I'm not a consultant who charges big bucks for managing other people's social media accounts. I'm not even that good with technology.

I'm a writer *just like you*—a busy person who needed to find a practical way to fit social media into her schedule so that it didn't take away from her writing or her family.

In the beginning, I didn't want to be on Twitter. I was one of the nay-sayers. I only joined because my brother, who at the time helped with a website design company for small businesses, told me that I needed to join if I wanted my blog to get any traffic. So I signed up, but I was never there. Basically, I tweeted twice a week when I had a new blog post up.

Months passed. I had five followers (and two of them were relatives), no traffic from Twitter, and no idea why it wasn't magically working for me. Yes, I was that naïve about social media.

In April 2011, the blog I ran with my friend Lisa Hall-Wilson got exactly 1,017 page views. We'd been blogging six months, and thinking we were nowhere near the 10,000 monthly page views agents consider a solid platform was depressing. Equally as depressing was that we also didn't have a strong enough platform if we decided to self-publish. Worse, we didn't know how to get more readers.

At a conference that month, we got a free 15-minute consult with a social media expert.

He asked me if I was on Twitter. Of course I was on Twitter.

"Are you using hashtags?" he asked.

I nodded, praying he wouldn't ask for details.

I didn't even know what a hashtag was.

I didn't know I could use something other than twitter.com to tweet. I didn't know how to meet new people on Twitter.

That conversation made me realize I didn't know how to use Twitter at all. And I was scared because I didn't know how I was going to find the time to do all the social media things I just found out I needed to do alongside blogging and improving my craft and finishing my novel and balancing the commitments of my non-writing life.

I wanted to cry. But after a lot of coffee and even more jelly beans, I sat down with Google, determined to figure out Twitter if it killed me. And I was sure it would.

I read everything I could find on Twitter and slowly figured it out through trial and error, because most of what you find online about Twitter is targeted to regular businesses, not writers. And there's a difference when it comes to using Twitter well.

By the end of 2012, I had over 5,600 followers, had developed friendships with some amazing people, and had turned Twitter into the #1 referral source for my blog. That year I started teaching other writers how to successfully use Twitter (and haven't stopped since), and now I'm putting what I've learned and taught into this book so I can hopefully help you as well.

But remember that fear I talked about—how am I going to do all this social media stuff and still find time to write and live my life?

Read on. That's where my philosophy about social media comes in.

PART ONE

Getting Started

CHAPTER ONE

A Philosophy of Social Media

If you've read any of my other Busy Writer's Guides, then you know I try to take a topic and cover it as comprehensively yet succinctly as possible in order to ease the learning curve for you. I do it because I understand that most of us already feel overwhelmed by our commitments and pulled in too many directions. This book might be about Twitter rather than about an element of writing craft, but my approach to it is the same.

As you work through this book, you will be investing time up-front to get properly set up and learn how to use Twitter. There's no way around putting in the time to learn, but this book will make sure you don't have to do it by trial and error the way I did. It'll also make sure you don't fall into the trap of doing Twitter wrong—which would be even worse because then the time you spent is wasted. So that up-front investment of time will pay off by making the long-term maintenance of your Twitter platform easier and (hopefully!) enjoyable.

In other words, we're going to work on building a Twitter platform that's sustainable for busy people.

For that to be possible, though, I need to explain my philosophy of social media to you because it's the foundation of everything else I'm going to teach you in this book.

Principle #1: Spamming people guarantees failure.

If you've come to this book looking for tips on how to automate every aspect of Twitter so that you don't have to think about it and so that your account automatically tweets out links to your blog or updates about your latest book, you won't find it here. If that's all you're willing to do on Twitter, find another book.

I'm not going to teach you how to do that because spamming people doesn't work. All spamming people and automating every-thing does is annoy people. Annoyed people aren't going to buy your books.

What we need to do instead is follow Principle #2.

Principle #2: Give before expecting to receive.

Let's be really honest with each other here. If you picked up this book, you did it because you want to use Twitter to build your au-thor platform and sell books.

And there's nothing wrong with that.

Where writers get into trouble having this as their goal is when they make Twitter all about them. All they talk about is their blog or their book. It becomes the "all-about-me-all-the-time" channel.

It's a selfish approach. We want people to give us their time, at-tention, and money, but we haven't given them any reason to. We don't really care about them, so why should they care about us?

We need to care about them first. Social media is social. It's about human beings connecting in a new way. It's about sharing and having conversations. It's about answering questions and helping find solutions.

Or at least it should be.

Care about what's going on in other people's lives. Answer their questions. Share valuable links and information.

Our approach to social media, even when our big-picture goal is to build a platform and sell books, needs to be about giving to others before we expect to receive anything from them.

Principle #3: Being successful on social media shouldn't require sacrificing large chunks of your writing or family time.

As I've already said, you'll have to invest time up-front learning to use Twitter, but after that, social media shouldn't be something that requires giving up most of your writing time or cutting in on your time with your family. If it takes away a lot of your writing time, your family time, or all of your recreation time, it's not sustainable. You'll eventually quit because the cost is too high. Writing is great, but we need a life outside of it and away from our computers.

A few minutes a day on Twitter where you interact authentically with other people and try to help them is all it takes to build a strong, thriving following there.

The more time you put in, the quicker your Twitter following will grow, but sustainability is key.

Principle #4: We all get further by working together and helping each other.

One of the reasons we can build a social media platform without sacrificing large chunks of our writing or family time is that we don't need to be on every social media site to succeed. When we, as writers, work together, we can do much more than any of us could do individually. You don't need to be on every site because someone else who enjoys your work is. Trust them to share it there. As we all work together, our reach magnifies.

A large part of what I'm going to recommend you do is help others, believing that, in turn, they'll help you. Tweet others' blog posts. Recommend books by other writers. Build up other people.

You'll reap what you sow, and others will do the same for you.

KRISTEN LAMB AND THE W.A.N.A. WAY

If you've been around the online writing community for any length of time, by now this philosophy of social media might sound familiar. It's because my approach to social media is also called the W.A.N.A. way, spearheaded by Kristen Lamb.

W.A.N.A. is an acronym meaning We Are Not Alone, and it's founded on genuine relationships rather than marketing tricks. Kristen called it the Love Revolution and wrote, "The Internet can be a scary place if you are doing this by yourself. Well, now you don't have to. We are going to be your adoptive Internet family...your Twibe."

In the past couple of years, Kristen has become a valued friend, and she encouraged me to write this book to help other writers navigate the Twitter waters. (I also recommend that you check out her book *Rise of the Machines: Human Authors in a Digital World*, as well as the classes taught at W.A.N.A. International. Full Disclosure: I also teach classes through W.A.N.A. International. If you'd like to take a class from me, check out the current listings at www.wanaintl.com.)

But I don't recommend doing things the W.A.N.A. way because Kristen and I are friends. I recommend it because it works.

And if all I could say about these methods is that they work, that'd probably be enough reason for many writers to want to learn them. But for me, personally, this is also about more. It's about being able to both succeed in my career and be the kind of person I want to be. Too often we're told that we need to compete with other writers to succeed. We need to beat others in order to win. We need to do it all. But that's not the case.

If you'll forgive my nerdiness, let me give you an illustration from *Star Trek*.

In the three-part opener of *Star Trek: Deep Space Nine*'s second season, the planet Bajor is on the brink of civil war thanks to an insurgent group known as The Circle.

Benjamin Sisko, commander of the Starfleet-controlled space station orbiting Bajor, brings important information to the general of the Bajoran military about who might be supplying weapons to the insurgents. It's helpful information the general needs in order to minimize the amount of Bajoran blood spilled.

Afterward, Sisko asks a favor. He tells the general it would mean a lot to him to have the Bajoran Major Kira returned to her position as the Bajoran liaison officer to the space station. (Kira was replaced against her and Sisko's wishes a few weeks earlier.)

The general claims he can't do anything about getting Kira reassigned back to the space station and turns away. But then he stops.

"Commander Sisko, you told me about the Kressari before you asked the favor regarding Kira. You could have tried to trade that information for the favor."

Sisko smiles. "I wouldn't do that."

"I'll remember that about you," the general says.

Sisko helped the general with no guarantee he'd get anything in return. He didn't even try to get anything in return.

He did what he did because it was the right thing to do, and because it showed the general the kind of man he was. Later, when success or failure came down to the general believing Sisko's word and helping him in return, Sisko's earlier actions made all the difference.

W.A.N.A. helps writers do the same thing. We give first, expecting nothing in return, because it's the right thing to do and it's the kind of people we want to be. And someday, when we need them, all the friends we make will be there for us.

I know it's true because it worked for me and for other writers I've met, worked with, and seen succeed.

So let's get started.

CHAPTER TWO

Getting Signed Up and Set Up on Twitter

Even if you have a Twitter account already, I recommend that you go through the next chapters anyway. It's not enough to just have an account. You need to be sure your account is set up properly.

Because Twitter, like all social media sites, is constantly changing, these chapters aren't accompanied by a lot of screenshots. What I've chosen to focus on instead are the principles that will stay consistent no matter how many times Twitter mutates. I want this book to give you the foundation you need to adapt to whatever comes.

Let's get started.

SIGN UP FOR AN ACCOUNT

Go to www.twitter.com and find the *Sign Up or New to Twitter?* box.

Twitter will want three pieces of information about you.

Piece #1: Your Full Name

Use your real name. Your name is part of your brand, and the more often people see it, the more likely they are to remember it.

I already hear possible objections. Alright, let me set your mind at ease.

But what if I want to work under a pseudonym?

I'm going to turn the question around on you. Why do you want to write under a pen name?

I don't want anyone to know who I really am.

Privacy on the Internet is an illusion. Even if you change everything else, you'll need to use a picture of your face not only for Twitter, but also on your website, on Facebook, on any other social media sites you use, and, eventually, on books. Someone will figure out who you really are, especially if you become famous, and then it's game over. You might as well be up-front from the beginning.

If you think that what you're writing will hurt your "day job" career or your family, or that it will endanger your safety, you need to stop and think about whether it's worth it. A pen name can't protect you forever.

I'm afraid I'll fail.

A surprising number of writers want to use a pen name in case they fail. They either don't want their friends and family to know about their writing unless they're successful or they want a back-up plan if the first books fail. If the first books fail, they figure they can switch names and start over. That's much more difficult to do if you've put your real name on those first books.

I never want to minimize anyone's fear. Writing is hard, and it is scary. But writing is also the kind of job where you sometimes need to take away the safety net in order to succeed. If you're using a pen name because you're afraid of failure, you're actually planning to fail rather than to succeed. You're also giving yourself an excuse to write less than your best or to publish before you're ready. And you've made it so that if you do succeed, you won't get to see your real name on the cover of that book. You'll be locked in to writing under a pen name.

Beyond that, you're not giving your friends and family the opportunity to support you if you hide what you're doing from them.

If this is your reason for choosing a pen name, give yourself a little time before you commit to it. Decisions made in fear are rarely the right ones.

(For more on cutting your safety net, take a look at my post on "The Dark Knight Rises: Is Your Safety Net Hurting You?")

My name is too boring.

So what? The name Dan Brown isn't exactly exciting. It didn't stop him from writing successful books. It's not how exciting your name is that will make you memorable. It's how well people connect with your content.

Are there any good reasons to use pen names?

Of course there are. Pen names aren't always bad or wrong, but make sure it's a conscious decision you're making for the right reasons. I'll walk you through the reasons you might legitimately want to use a pen name.

All the virtual real estate around your real name is already taken.

You might find that someone has already snatched up the website URL, Facebook URL, Twitter username, etc. for your real name.

In that case, the answer may be as simple as adding "author" to the end. For example, my website URL is www.marcykennedy.com. If that was already taken, I could have gone with www.marcykennedyauthor.com. Even if your name is common, you're still probably the only writer with your name who has a website.

If you're not, consider some variation of your name. Use your first and middle initials rather than your first name. Add a middle initial along with your first name. Play with the spelling of your first name. If the real spelling of my name had been taken, I could have used Marci or Marcie or Marcey.

My friend Lisa Hall-Wilson decided to go with a hyphenated last name (a combination of her married name and maiden name) because her name was so common almost every other possible variation was taken.

However you go about it, this will be easier to remember and maintain if you're using your real name or some variation on it. For more suggestions on using variations of your name to write under and whether you should, check out Jami Gold's post "Branding 101: To Pen Name or Not to Pen Name."

Your name doesn't fit your genre.

Romance sells better with a woman's name on the cover. Hard science fiction sells better with a man's name on the cover. Marketability is why J. K. Rowling used J. K. rather than Joanne. If you're picking a pen name as a marketing strategy, okay. In this case, you'll likely use your pen name for all your social media and have your real name somewhere on your website.

Your name is identical or almost identical to a bestselling author.

Remember how I used Dan Brown as an example earlier? If you happen to be named Dan Brown, James Patterson, Steven King, Nora Roberts, Stephanie Meyer, or any other name that's very similar to a bestselling author, a pen name might be a wise choice.

Your name is unintentionally funny or almost impossible to spell correctly.

You want people to be able to at least come close to the correct spelling of your name when they do an internet or bookstore search for you or your book. For example, my maternal grandparents were born in Czechoslovakia. Last names from that part of the world tend to combine consonants and vowels in a way that's difficult for North American English speakers to handle. If I'd inherited the last name Hlavin, Kohoutek, or Prochazka, I would have seriously considered using a pen name to make it easier for people to not only find me but also tell their friends about my books.

If you already write under multiple names, should you set up multiple Twitter accounts?

The simple answer is *no*. Multiple Twitter accounts are a fast track to crazy and to turning into a spam bot. It's hard enough to properly maintain social media accounts for one personality, let alone for many. If you write under multiple names, use your real name for your Twitter account and explain all your pseudonyms to people on your website/blog. You'll lose a little name recognition, but that's better than ending up with multiple Twitter accounts that you don't have time to actively use.

If you still decide after all this that you want to work under a single pen name, then that pen name should be what you use on Twitter and everywhere else on your social media platform, including your website URL. Consistency is foundational when it comes to building a brand.

Piece #2: Your Email

Choose an email address that you use regularly because you'll want to see notifications when they come in. Pretty self-explanatory, right?

Piece #3: Your Password

Choose a password that you don't use anywhere else. It will need to be six characters or more in length, and I strongly recommend using a combination of letters, numbers and special characters. You can also vary the case of your letters. We'll be talking more about passwords later, in the chapter on online safety.

Once you click the button to sign up, you'll be taken to a page where Twitter will check the information you've entered. They'll email you a confirmation to confirm that you entered your email address correctly and they'll check that you've entered a long enough password.

This is also where you'll need to choose a username.

DECIDE ON YOUR USERNAME

Your username is important because it will show up when people send you a tweet, when they retweet anything you tweet, etc. It's what you'll be known by on Twitter.

For example, my username is @MarcyKennedy.

The best choice for your username is simply your name. The more often people see your name, the more likely they'll be to remember it when they go to a bookstore or are about to search Amazon for a great new book to read.

What if my name isn't available as a username?

You still have options.

You can include an underscore between your first and last name (e.g., Marcy_Kennedy).

You can add *writer* to the end (e.g., MarcyKennedyWriter).

You can add the abbreviation of your state/province behind your name (e.g., MarcyKennedyON).

Be creative, but do your best to try to get your full first name and full last name in. If you can't, or if your name is simply too long to be practical (the shorter the username, the better for leaving plenty of room for the tweet itself), include your full last name and abbreviate your first name.

Now read the terms of service, and then click the button to create your account.

TAILORING TWITTER TO YOUR RECENT WEBSITE VISITS

On the same signup page, you'll see two check boxes at the bottom. One offers to keep you signed in to Twitter and the other offers the option to "Tailor Twitter based on my recent website visits."

If you agree to this, basically what happens is they analyze the websites you've visited that have a Twitter button integrated into them and then suggest people for you to follow based on who other people who've visited that same site are following.

This is something you can join, but I don't recommend it. Automated algorithms like this are rarely accurate and even more rarely helpful. But there's another issue involved that I'll talk about in just a minute when I explain why you want to ignore Twitter's attempts to have you follow people.

IGNORE TWITTER'S ATTEMPTS TO HAVE YOU FOLLOW PEOPLE

Once you've created your account, Twitter will take you through a series of set-up steps.

Eventually you'll reach a page where Twitter prompts you to build your timeline by following five people from a list of suggestions. **Don't do it.** You want to skip this step.

But why do I want to skip this step?

First of all, if you're spending your time on Twitter reading tweets from Ashton Kutcher or Pink, you probably need to reevaluate your time management skills.

On a more practical level, you shouldn't be following anyone at all until you finish filling out your profile. Right now, you have no picture and no bio, which means you look like a spam bot. No one will follow you back when you look like a spam bot.

You also need to be a little strategic about your numbers when you first sign up. If you go crazy and follow 100 people but you only have five people following you, it works as social proof against you. Every new person you follow will look at those numbers and think "I wonder why no one wants to follow them. Maybe I shouldn't either."

We'll get you to the point where you can basically follow whoever you want (because one of the joys of Twitter is being able to follow the tweets of some of the big names), but you need to be patient for the moment.

What if Twitter won't let me skip this step?

This is one part of Twitter that's always changing. If Twitter won't let you skip any of the steps I suggest you skip, then simply follow five people and unfollow them as soon as you're set up. Believe me, the famous people won't even notice.

To unfollow them, as soon as your account is set up, click on ***Following*** under your profile picture. It'll take you to a new page. If you hover your mouse curser over the big blue ***Following*** square next to each of their names, you'll see it turn red and say ***Unfollow***. Unfollowing is as simple as clicking in that spot.

Twitter is also going to ask if you want them to search your contacts in the email address you provided to connect you with people you already know who are on Twitter.

If you think these people will know it's you simply by your name (remember, you don't have a picture or a bio yet), then you can go through with this step if you want. My recommendation, though, is that you skip this step as well. You can always add these people later.

Twitter will often make the ***Skip*** option very difficult to see. Usually you can find it at the very bottom of the box where they list the email clients (e.g., Gmail, Yahoo, Hotmail, AOL). It'll be in tiny gray font on a gray background.

Once you either follow a few people or skip the step, you'll finally have reached the good stuff—adding a picture and your bio.

CHOOSE A PROFILE PICTURE

Your picture needs to be a picture of you, preferably a close-up of your face.

The trick to this is that you only have 700KB. The pictures I take on my digital camera generally average between 900 KB and 1.5 MB. Professional photos are often bigger than 10 MB.

It's actually easy to fix. I'm going to walk you through it using Paint because it comes already installed on any Windows operating systems. If you're using a Mac, you'll have to find a similar program.

(If you're using a Mac, you probably know much more about graphic design than I do and you don't even need these instructions.)

If your computer didn't come with Paint for some reason, you can download a free program, PAINT.net. It's a fancier program that's an open-source alternative to Photoshop, but it will let you do the same thing, and you don't have to worry about its bells and whistles if you don't want to. You can download PAINT.net at www.getpaint.net.

Now, open Paint and open your photo. (If you can't seem to find Paint, look in the Accessories folder of your Start menu.)

Rename your photo and save it as a JPEG before you do anything else. You probably want to keep the original as-is. If the photo isn't a close up of your face, crop it. Paint makes cropping easy. You use the *Select* button, and then once you've outlined the part you want to keep, you click *Crop* (it's directly to the left of the big Select option).

Done? Okay, on we go.

Underneath where it said *Crop*, click *Resize*.

Make sure that *Maintain Aspect Ratio* is selected so that your face doesn't get warped out of shape, then select *Pixels*.

If your picture is taller than it is wide, type *970* into the vertical box. If your picture is wider than it is tall, type *970* into the horizontal box. (Ignore the *Skew* portion of the box entirely.)

Save again, and then upload it to Twitter.

The next step is adding your bio.

THE BIO – MORE COMPLEX THAN IT LOOKS

For now, just put whatever you want in the bio box. In Chapter Six, we're going to look at how to write a strong bio in only 160 characters.

Now that we've reached the end, some of you might be panicking.

What do I do if I already have an account, but I didn't make my username my name or I have a picture that's not a close-up of my face?

No need to worry. Twitter always allows you to change these at any time. All you need to do is go to *Settings* (currently accessible from the dropdown menu by the gear symbol at the top right of the page).

You can change your username under *Account* and your picture under *Profile*.

CHAPTER THREE

How to Set Your Notifications

You're almost done getting Twitter set up. And once we get all this out of the way, we can get to the fun stuff.

Many of the settings are going to be personal preference (for example, language and time zone). What I'm going to go through are the settings that are important to you for either professional or safety reasons.

Sign in to Twitter, and go back to the *Settings* area. In case you missed it in the last chapter, to find *Settings*, click on the gear symbol that's usually found at the top right-hand side of the page once you're signed in.

ACCOUNT SETTINGS

Currently when you go to *Settings*, you're already on the *Account* tab. If not, select it from the menu on the left. This is where you can change your username or the email attached to your account, but there are also other items here you need to take care of.

Content Containing Sensitive Material

Sensitive content is defined by Twitter as nudity, violence, or medical procedures. If you mark your content as containing sensitive content, people will get a warning that they'll need to click through before seeing your material.

If people have clicked the "display media that may contain sensitive content," they won't see a warning.

Honestly, even if you're an erotica author, you shouldn't be tweeting this sort of material. Plus, you can't mark only some of your material as sensitive, so you're better off not tweeting sensitive material at all.

If you are going to share sensitive media, please click this box to warn people. It's the right thing to do.

Save your changes. If you don't do this, all that work will be lost.

SECURITY AND PRIVACY

This is the next tab in your menu, and we have work to do here as well.

Login Verification and Password Reset

In an attempt to help you protect your account, Twitter now offers increased security measures for when you login or want to change your password. Whether or not you decide to do these is up to you. If you always have your cell phone with you when you want to log in, then it's smart to take every precaution you can.

Tweet Privacy/Protection

Do **NOT** protect your tweets.

If you protect your tweets, you're going to lose a lot of potential followers. Most people won't go through the extra step of asking for permission to follow you. The point of social media is to be accessible.

But what if I want to keep what I'm tweeting private?

Then you shouldn't be tweeting it. I've said it before, but I'll keep saying it—privacy on social media is an illusion. Never tweet anything you'd be uncomfortable with the world (or your parents or spouse or boss) seeing.

Tweet Location

Make sure this box is *NOT* selected.

You don't want to be tying a location to any of your tweets. (This is also why you shouldn't be using Foursquare.)

Why?

It's a safety issue. You don't want people knowing when you're away from home. It's like advertising to criminals that your home is empty and waiting for them. You also don't want to tell the world where you are. You might never have trouble with an over-zealous fan or a stalker, but it's better to be wise than sorry. More on this later.

Save your changes.

EMAIL NOTIFICATION SETTINGS

Part of the challenge you're going to face with all social media is how to manage your time. We're going to get into that in more detail later, but this is one of my tricks—I make sure Twitter tells me when anything important happens.

You can do this under the *Activity Related to You and Your Tweets* heading.

Check the boxes to have Twitter notify you when

- your tweets are marked as favorites *by anyone*,

- your tweets are retweeted *by anyone*,
- your tweets get a reply or you're mentioned in a tweet *by anyone*,
- you're followed by someone new, or
- you're sent a direct message.

By having notifications sent directly to my inbox, I'm more able to be interactive without having to keep Twitter (or TweetDeck or Hootsuite) open all day.

You don't have to respond to the emails from Twitter the moment they come in if you find this distracting. I usually store them up, and it only takes me a couple of minutes when I take a break to follow new people and respond to tweets that have come in.

Now, because I know you probably still have questions...

Why do you want to know when your tweets are marked as favorites or retweeted by anyone (rather than just by people you follow)?

First of all, this lets you see who is interacting with and interested in your content. These are great people to get to know better. Send them a thank you, retweet something of theirs, or start a conversation. If you're not already following them, follow them.

Why do I want to know when my tweets get a reply or I'm mentioned in a tweet?

These are conversations. These people want to talk to you (or are talking about you/your content). For a long time, I had this marked as "people I follow." I was missing out on getting to know new people.

Why do I want to receive an email when I'm followed by someone new?

So you can decide whether or not to follow them back.

Why do I want to receive an email when I'm sent a direct message?

A direct message is a "private" message between you and the person sending it. You can only receive them if you're both following each other.

When you sign up for TweetDeck or Hootsuite, you can have a column for these, but I find they're too easy to miss that way. Direct messages are important because someone is trying to communicate directly with you.

I've had people let me know if my website server went down. I've had people tell me about broken links. I've carried on private conversations. I've exchanged email addresses. DMs are valuable. You don't want to risk missing them.

Save your changes. Just one more settings tab to go in this chapter.

PROFILE SETTINGS

You've filled in most of this already, but there are a couple of things you still need to fill in. For now, don't worry about your header (the box under your profile picture). We'll get to that later.

Your Location

This should be a real location. Don't say Neverland. Or Outer Space. Or anything else that seems witty to you in the moment.

You're trying to reassure people that you're a real person. Plus, by adding a location, you'll be better able to connect with other writers and eventually fans in your area. (And anything you think is wildly creative has probably been used before.)

However, you also need to stay safe.

If you looked at my Twitter profile, you'd see that I give my province and country. I don't tell you my town (and I certainly don't tell you my street) because I come from a small town. If you live in a big city like New York or Dallas, you're safe to put your city if you want to. Be smart and only give as much information as you're comfortable with.

Your Website/Blog Address

This is why you don't have to put your blog or website address in your bio in the chapter on writing your Twitter bio. Twitter already has a spot for it, so you don't need to waste those precious characters.

This is one of the most important fields to fill in. If new followers want to check you out, you want them to be able to.

You'd be surprised how many new followers I chat with and then can't support with a link to some of their content because they don't give me this information.

Connect to Facebook

Twitter gives you the option to connect Twitter and Facebook, so that all your tweets post to Facebook as well. This can seem like a great time-saving option on the surface. But Facebook is not Twitter.

Do not post your tweets to Facebook!

I'm sorry for being repetitive, but I feel the need to say this again.

Do not post your tweets to Facebook! And if you already have them linked, go unlink them. Fast!

Consider this button a bug zapper—and you're the bug. No touching.

Facebook has a different culture to it.

You shouldn't post as often on Facebook as you do on Twitter. On Twitter, it's common to post every hour, sometimes multiple times per hour. On Facebook, you want to post three to four times a day max. If people look at their newsfeed and your page or profile is monopolizing it, you're going to get blocked, unliked, or unfriended.

People are looking for different kinds of posts on Facebook in terms of length than Twitter allows.

People on Facebook don't like repetition in posts. On Twitter, it's okay if you post the same link twice in a day as long as you do it at different times. With how fast columns move and people's different schedules, you aren't likely to have the same people see it twice.

Linking them also tells people that you're never on Facebook. Why should they give you their time to read and respond to your status updates if you can't be bothered to do the same?

This is just really bad social media etiquette all around. Don't cross-post.

Save your changes.

What do I do if I have Twitter and Facebook linked already?!

It's a simple enough fix, but you have to make sure you disable it on both ends. You'll change it on Twitter in the spot we looked at above, and you also need to disable the app on Facebook. If you don't fix it in both locations, your tweets will keep appearing in Facebook.

Now that we have all the basics out of the way, we can move on to writing our bio and designing our Twitter profile and custom header.

CHAPTER FOUR

How to Design Your Twitter Page

Many of us who are writers also love visual beauty. This is your chance to let those other creative instincts out to play.

Twitter is notorious for changing this particular feature. Even if the specifics change, all the principles in this chapter will still apply.

However, I know that some of you reading this will have the "old" version where you could add an image to your Twitter page's background and won't want to switch to the new version where your image just has an image banner at the top. If that's the case, after you read this chapter (because you'll want a custom header regardless of which version you have), you can jump to Appendix A to read about customizing your background.

For those of you who have the new version, read on. We're going to talk about creating your custom header.

Go back to **Settings** and choose the **Profile** tab.

CREATING YOUR CUSTOM HEADER

Currently, on the *Profile* page, under where you can change your picture, you're also given the option to change your header. This is where you want to invest the real time for one very important reason. Since Twitter acquired TweetDeck, they've been making some smart updates to both their home site and to the way TweetDeck and Twitter interact. The header you choose here will show up in your TweetDeck profile, as well as on your Twitter profile page.

(If you just had a heart attack because you don't know what TweetDeck is, no worries. You don't need to know what TweetDeck is to create your custom header, and I have a whole chapter on TweetDeck and Hootsuite later on.)

Without a custom header, here's what your profile page looks like.

With a custom header, here's what your profile page looks like.

Marcy Kennedy
@MarcyKennedy
Fantasy writer, freelance editor, Great Dane owner, and jelly bean connoisseur.
I look for hope in the darkness. And I tweet a lot.
Ontario, Canada · marcykennedy.com/blog

It's more visually appealing.

Other than visual appeal, why is this custom header such a big deal?

People who are using TweetDeck see it when they click on your name in TweetDeck. This means that, unlike your profile background in the old version of Twitter, it will be seen. Every time someone wants to see your bio or click on your website link to see if they can return the favor of an RT of your content, they'll see this header. Some people also click on your name to add you to lists, see what lists you've created, check out who's mentioned you, etc.

In the new version of Twitter, this header is also what appears at the top of your profile page if people actually go there.

The custom header is a valuable piece of real estate.

Unfortunately, you don't have a lot of space, so you need to use it well.

Pick an image that represents your brand.

If you write werewolf novels, you could find an image of a wolf in the forest. If you write legal thrillers, you could find an image of a courtroom scene, with a gavel dripping with blood. If you write chick lit, you might simply choose a great pair of shoes. Whatever it is, it should say something about your brand. I write fantasy, so to keep my branding consistent across platforms, I've used the same custom background of a foreign sky with multiple moons, close planets, and a castle on a hill that I use on my website.

Since the text of your bio is white, the darker/richer the image you choose, the better. It helps your bio stand out.

Be aware of where your headshot appears in the image.

You can't move the location of your headshot at this time, so you don't want anything important in your header image to disappear behind it. (Although, if the image you upload for your custom header is bigger or smaller than 1252 × 626, you are able to move your background image around and zoom in or out.)

The unchangeable placement of your headshot, along with the white text of your bio, is one of the reasons the custom header isn't the best place for your book cover. If you want to put your book cover in your custom header, then you can create a background of 1252 × 626 in a complementary color and paste a smaller image of your cover into the corners, using a program like Paint. You'll have to play around with the size of each image to see what you like.

You could also use a portion of your cover art as your custom header rather than your whole book cover. (See the custom header of author Nathan Farrugia as an example. Every time he releases a new book, he updates this custom header to use a piece of the cover.)

Don't add your name or website address into the custom header.

Your name is already prominently displayed. Your website link is already listed and clickable. While it might be tempting to list these things again, you need to be aware of making the space too cluttered.

What you really want to achieve with this custom header is making your brand interesting and memorable. If you want to add words to your custom header, a better use of the space would be for a tagline if you have one.

My tagline is "Fantasy is more real than you think..." Part of my brand is that I take fantasy and science fiction and show how we can learn lessons from it that apply to life. I write fantasy that (I hope) even non-fantasy fans will enjoy because of the deeper themes and emotions running through it.

My friend Lisa Hall-Wilson uses the tagline "Blogging through the fire." It's in the header of her blog and on her Facebook profile. It represents her brand because she faces the dirty, ugly truths in life in the belief that the truth sets you free. She wants to help people walk through the flames and come out the other side. She uses the same image in her custom header as on her blog and Facebook page.

We're going to talk more about representing our brands on Twitter when we talk about bios.

Your custom header will work best if it's at least 1252 × 626. The file can be no bigger than 5 MB.

It may not upload properly the first time.

Occasionally, an internal server error on Twitter's end will mean that your custom header doesn't upload. You haven't done anything wrong. Give it a second try. If it still doesn't work, leave it and come back later. It should upload perfectly when you do.

If you've updated to the new look in Twitter, you can also update your header by clicking on *Me* from the top navigation bar and then clicking on **Edit Profile**. (You'll also notice that this is an alternate way to update your profile picture, you bio, your location, and your website URL.)

Very few people do these design elements of Twitter well. When you do, you'll immediately stand out as more professional and interesting.

CHAPTER FIVE

Essential Terminology

Before we go any further, I need to make sure that you know the basic terminology so that we'll be on the same page. I'll try to refresh your memory the first time a term is used in later chapters, but if you're not sure, check back here.

Tweets

These are the messages or status updates you send on Twitter. You have a maximum of 140 characters, including spaces and punctuation. These are public and are seen by everyone on Twitter who follows you or anyone who looks at your profile.

Tweeps

Tweeps are your friends on Twitter. You'll see all kinds of variations on this, like *tweeple*.

Followers

Unlike on Facebook, where you make friends or like someone's page, people on Twitter follow you. When they follow you, your tweets will show up in their Twitter stream. (I'll explain streams soon.) If you follow them, their tweets will show up in yours. You don't have to give approval when someone follows you, and you're not obligated to follow them back (though it's polite to do so if you might have something in common with them). In a later lesson, we'll look at what to do if someone follows you and you don't want them to.

Reply

Both Hootsuite and TweetDeck make replying to a tweet easy. All you have to do is hit the button that looks like an arrow that appears when you hover over the tweet you want to reply to.

Retweets

Retweets are when you tweet something someone else tweeted first. You can retweet something you find funny or a link someone else shares.

So if I tweet...

Four Fiction Felonies that Make Your Plot Unbelievable *http://wp.me/p3h9G6-Pn*

You would write...

RT @MarcyKennedy Four Fiction Felonies that Make Your Plot Unbelievable *http://wp.me/p3h9G6-Pn*

It's considered rude to take someone else's tweet as your own without giving them credit with an RT.

A new variation of the RT is the MT. Not everyone bothers with this, but an MT is a modified tweet. It means you're retweeting someone, but you've made major changes to their tweet in order to fit the character limit.

You can manually retweet someone by copying their message into the compose box and writing out the RT @username, but that's tedious.

In both TweetDeck and Hootsuite (which we'll learn about next), you can easily retweet by pressing the symbol that's two arrows making a square (a lot like a recycling symbol) that will appear when you hover your mouse over a tweet.

In both programs, you can either retweet it as is or edit it first. You're almost always going to choose to edit.

@ Mentions

The @ symbol is how you send a tweet to someone on Twitter. If you wanted to tweet me, you'd write @MarcyKennedy (no space between the @ and my username) and then write your message.

The location of your @ matters. Let's look at an example. Say you wanted to tweet me about meeting for coffee.

@MarcyKennedy Want to grab a coffee this afternoon?

This message is only seen by you, me, and anyone who follows both of us. There's a good reason for this. It ensures that, when you're having a conversation with someone on Twitter, you don't clog up all of your followers' streams with something they won't be interested in.

What if we reversed the order?

Want to grab a coffee this afternoon, @MarcyKennedy?

Everyone who follows you sees this tweet.

When you're sending a message you intend for only one person, use the first option.

When you're thanking someone for a retweet, use the first option. If you use the second option, it can look a little manipulative because it's like you want everyone who follows you to know how many other people are retweeting your content.

Direct Messages

These are private messages sent to a single person on Twitter. You still have the 140-character limit.

Direct messages are called DMs. You can send a direct message by writing *DM username* and then your message. Programs like TweetDeck also allow you to send a DM by clicking on a user or their message. (Again, more on that later.)

You can only send a direct message to someone who is following you and who you also follow. Twitter does this as a way to protect you from spam.

Hashtags

A hashtag is the # sign followed by a term.

Hashtags get your tweet in front of people even if they aren't following you because people can create columns in a program like TweetDeck or Hootsuite to follow hashtags that interest them.

For example, if you write a tweet and add the #MyWANA hashtag to the end, anyone who has created a column to follow that hashtag will see your tweet. We'll spend an entire chapter on hashtags.

You should add a hashtag to most of your tweets because it helps you connect with people, but never add more than two or three. Twitter (and most users) consider more than three hashtags to be spam.

#FF

This hashtag stands for *Follow Friday*. It's a way to suggest to your followers other people they might want to follow. There's a right and a wrong way to do this.

The wrong way (although you see it a lot) is to gather up as many usernames as will fit in a tweet and #FF them.

The right way is to choose one or two people to #FF and tell your followers something great about them. Why should they follow them?

A variation of #FF is #WW. #WW stands for *Writer Wednesday*. The purpose is the same, but more specific. Suggest other writers people should be following.

CHAPTER SIX

How to Write Your Twitter Bio

Despite being writers, we're often lazy when it comes to writing a good Twitter bio. But we can't afford to be.

WHY IS YOUR TWITTER BIO SO IMPORTANT?

When you follow someone, your Twitter bio is the first thing they see in the notification email.

First impressions matter, even on Twitter.

Think about how busy you are. If you're getting 10, 15, 20 people a day following you, will you have time to read past tweets on people who have a terrible bio? Would you even bother? A lot of people won't. You'll either get a follower or get deleted based on your bio.

Your Twitter bio helps people decide whether you're a real person or a spam bot.

Follower counts aren't always a good way to tell a real person from a spam bot because many spam bots will follow 1,000 people, then unfollow them all, knowing that a certain percentage have their accounts set to auto-follow. (Setting your account to auto-follow is a bad idea, and we'll talk about it more in the chapter on automation.)

Do you see how difficult that makes it if you don't have a clear bio?

One of the quickest ways to get ignored on Twitter is to seem like you're not a real person.

People will find you in searches based on the words you use in your Twitter bio.

You want to be found on Twitter, so make it easier for people by using keywords. This is why you want to include things like your genre in your bio, as well as some of your interests.

HOW DO YOU CREATE A BIO THAT MAKES A GREAT FIRST IMPRESSION?

Well, unlike the bio on your website, it comes with an extra challenge.

You only have 160 characters to write your Twitter bio, including spaces and punctuation. Not sure how long that is? This bolded paragraph is 162 characters long.

That's not a lot of space to make a lasting impression and to do it without using a lot of unintelligible abbreviations.

The trick with your Twitter bio is to balance the three P's - *professional*, *personable*, and *personality-filled*.

A bio can be solid without including all three, but the best bios use all of them.

Step #1: Tell people what you do.

If you're on Twitter to build your platform, this doesn't mean your day job (unless it's related to your books, like you're a lawyer who writes legal thrillers).

If you're a writer, this means what you write. A non-fiction book about what? What genre of novel?

Use first person.

Third person isn't wrong, but it adds a layer of distance. Since social media is supposed to be social and give people a way to get to know you and connect with you, why hold them at arm's length? It doesn't make you less professional to also be friendly and approachable.

You don't need to mention the title of your book(s).

I've never purchased a book based on a Twitter bio. I've never even clicked through to look at a book based on a Twitter bio. I have purchased books because I chatted with someone on Twitter and liked them. I've also purchased books based on the recommendations of people I've gotten to know on Twitter. This is about relationships.

If you have extra characters and want to include your book title, go ahead, but there are better ways to use those characters.

If you're repped by an agent, mention that, because it adds credibility. (This is actually better to include than the title of your book.) If you're an author with a single publisher (e.g., Random House, Simon & Shuster, Entangled, Marcher Lord Press) that's also something that's better to put in your bio than your book title, again because of the credibility factor.

So, for example, you could say "I'm a romantic suspense author with Love Inspired."

Step #2: Add something that shows your personality and lets people connect to you as a human being.

For example, I tell people I'm a Great Dane owner and a jelly bean connoisseur. I've had so many fun conversations start with people both through tweets and through direct messages about those two points. People tell me about their dogs (even if they've never met a Dane) or about Great Danes they've met in the past. They'll even tell me their favorite jelly bean flavors.

It breaks the ice.

It can be extremely difficult to know what to say to someone you've just followed on Twitter, so this gives them a helping hand.

Try to choose something non-writing-related.

I'll give you a couple more examples of bios where the person's personality shines through.

Example #1: Natalie Harford (@NatalieHartford)

Communications specialist, writer, blogger, urban redneck. Loves reality TV, golf and all things pink. If I owned a Be-Dazzler, I'd be dangerous.

If you were to follow Natalie, you could start up a conversation about reality TV or golf, or even about bling.

Example #2: Piper Bayard (@PiperBayard)

Author of post-apocalyptic sci fi & spy novels. Blogger, belly dancer, shooter, SCUBA diver, Hospice volunteer, recovering attorney.

Even if you've never read a spy novel or a post-apocalyptic sci-fi work, you could ask Piper about belly dancing or scuba diving, or you could swap volunteer experiences.

You don't need to devote a lot of space to this. It could be as simple as listing your favorite hobby or one other unique thing (e.g., you're gluten-free, you own a bearded dragon, you can juggle).

Step #3: What's the high-concept purpose in what you do?

This is connected to your brand. Your brand is your name + your genre + the promise you make to your audience about what they're going to get.

What this comes down to is why you're doing what you're doing. Why do you write? What excites you? What will you be able to connect with your readers on? What promise are you making them?

The best way I can explain this to you is to give you some examples.

Here's my Twitter bio:

> Fantasy writer, freelance editor, Great Dane owner, and jelly bean connoisseur. *I look for hope in the darkness.* And I tweet a lot.

I've bolded my high-concept purpose. This is the heart of what I do and why I do it. I want to tell stories that give people hope.

On the About page on my website, I expand on this:

> I'm a fantasy writer, freelance editor, and writing instructor who believes there's always hope. Sometimes you just have to dig a little harder to find it.
>
> In a world that can be dark and brutal and unfair, hope is one of our most powerful weapons. I write novels that encourage people to keep fighting. I want to

let them know that no one is beyond redemption and that, in the end, good always wins.

If you read my blog posts, you'll find the theme of hope running throughout all of them, as well. It's who I am. Who are you?

I'll give you another example from Lisa Hall-Wilson (@LisaHallWilson).

> I write dark fantasy fiction that's **bare your soul honest**. Freelance writer, dog-owning cat lover. I tweet, but I rock Facebook. CU there!

I've bolded her high-concept purpose.

Lisa has a different touch point with her audience. She calls herself a truth-teller.

Her bio says...

> Life has taught me that sometimes bad things happen, sometimes the bully wins, and sometimes no one hears no matter how loud you scream, but through my stories and articles - I have a voice. I blog Through The Fire because I'm convinced the truth sets you free.

If you read Lisa's blog or one of her future books, you're going to get a different experience from when you read my work. Lisa doesn't promise her readers a happy ending, or even a hopeful ending. She only promises them to paint an accurate picture (at least of how she sees it).

You don't necessarily have to be philosophical and esoteric in this, though.

Your brand might be light and fun. Perhaps you're catering to a specific group of people.

Take a look at Emmie Mears bio (@EmmieMears):

Urban fantasy writer. Saving the world from brooding one self-actualized vampire at a time. Creator of #ZAP, the Zombie Apocalypse Preparation Fitness Program.

Emmie is trying to breathe new life into vampire novels—no sparkling, no brooding. In other words, she's writing for people who love vampires but hated *Twilight*.

What if I don't know my purpose yet? What if I'm new?

You can change your Twitter bio at any time. For now, have fun.

I found this bio from Janet Taylor (@Janet_B_Taylor) and loved it.

I am one of those in the horrifying sub-class of people known as pre-published. Turn away—I'm hideous. Writer of YA Time Travel/Hisfic. Lover of cheese.

She's referencing a line from Harry Potter, almost like an inside joke for other fans.

She's since gotten an agent and has changed her Twitter bio. What you write here isn't set in stone. As your situation changes, your bio can change with it.

Isn't this a lot of work just for a Twitter bio?

Narrowing down your brand is hard work. You have to think about what ties your writing together and what type of audience you're hoping to reach. However, this isn't something you're doing just for Twitter. If you don't know your brand, you need to think about it for the sake of your career. Being able to put it in your Twitter bio is just a bonus. The idea of brand and what you want readers to walk away with is going to keep coming up.

WHAT SHOULDN'T YOU INCLUDE IN YOUR BIO?

Don't include politics, religion, or sexuality.

Unless you're writing a book about politics, for a particular faith population, or featuring characters of a particular sexual orientation, this is more likely to drive people away than to keep them because they'll be afraid you're going to get up on a soapbox and preach at them.

If you *are* writing particularly for one of those audiences, though, it's smart to include these in your bio. For example, if you're writing inspirational historical romance like Jody Hedlund does, then by all means include *Christian* in your Twitter bio. That's important for her readers to find her and identify with her.

Don't use hashtags in your bio.

Novelist of 5-star #fantasy #novel SKY DIAMOND available for #Kindle and #Nook. Passionate about #football, #dogs, and #running.

People do it because they know others are going to search for those terms, but you don't need to add a hashtag to show up in a search. Hashtags are meant for conversations, not bios.

Adding hashtags into your bio is tacky, and it makes it annoying for real humans to read. Your bio needs to be for people first and foremost.

Don't try to cram in everything and the kitchen sink— that makes you comes across as scattered.

Novelist. Bird owner. Cat owner. Wife. Mom. Reader. Online gameplayer. Loves jazz. Aspiring zombie killer. Trekkie. Marathon runner. Housecleaner.

Don't come off as arrogant.

My novel is a fantasy that will pull you in for more.

This kind of self-back-patting doesn't belong in your Twitter bio. If your work is great, your friends and fans will tell other people how awesome it is. You're better off showing a little humility.

If you're a bestselling author, however, don't be afraid to mention it. That's something you should be proud of. It's not bragging. It's not personal opinion. It's a fact and therefore belongs in your Twitter bio if you want to put it there.

WON'T I END UP WITH A BIO THAT'S TOO LONG?

Your first attempt at a bio will likely be too long. The idea is to write it out in a Word doc (or other word processing program where you can save it) and then play with it until you're able to say what you want in a limited space. It's actually a great exercise in writing tight.

CHAPTER SEVEN

TweetDeck vs. Hootsuite

W e've spent all this time setting up Twitter, but we're not actually going to use Twitter.com to tweet. It only gives you one column and very few options. You need something more effective to manage your tweeting.

You have two basic choices—TweetDeck and Hootsuite. (There are others, but these two are the best.)

You'll hear from people who love one or the other, so the important thing is to choose the one you like. I used to recommend TweetDeck. I now recommend Hootsuite. That could change in the future as both platforms make changes.

The great thing is that, because both are external applications that connect to your Twitter account, you don't lose anything by swapping between them. You could start with one if you want, decide you don't like it, and switch to the other one. All your followers and lists go with you. (Though you will have to customize the appearance of the new application.)

Much like in the first chapter where I walked you through signing up for Twitter, I want to start this chapter with the caution that social media applications and sites are constantly changing. I'm going to give you instructions on how to customize Hootsuite and Twitter, but I'm going to do it in such a way that, even if the platforms change something about the way they look, you'll still be able to get set up and comfortable with them. In other words, my focus is more on the general principles than it is on giving you a lot of screenshots to walk you through each detail of the way the platforms currently are.

So let's take a look at both to help you decide which one is right for you.

HOOTSUITE VS. TWEETDECK

One of the biggest advantages Hootsuite used to have over TweeDeck was that Hootsuite was online. You kept a tab open on your internet browser. TweetDeck was an application you down-loaded and installed on your hard drive.

In other words, Hootsuite was less resource-intensive. If you had an older computer or a computer with limited RAM, Hootsuite was the better choice for you. Hootsuite was also sometimes preferred if you were sharing a computer or if you used a laptop that tended to run hot. (You'd know it if you had one. You could set your coffee cup by where the air vented and it'd stay warm. Not so great when you wanted to actually put your laptop on your lap.)

TweetDeck has other advantages over Hootsuite.

TweetDeck sends tweets faster and updates more frequently so that you're communicating in real time.

Hootsuite also has advantages over TweetDeck.

At the present time, all support for mobile TweetDeck apps has been removed. In other words, if you want to access Twitter on something other than your regular computer or laptop, you'll need to use Hootsuite anyway. The termination of TweetDeck mobile apps has led to speculation about how long it will be before Twitter withdraws support for the online and desktop versions as well. This is the main reason I recommend Hootsuite.

Another reason I now recommend Hootsuite is that TweetDeck, as of May 2013, removed Facebook integration. In other words, the only thing TweetDeck is good for is monitoring Twitter. On Hootsuite, you can monitor both your Facebook and Twitter accounts.

TweetDeck and Hootsuite once had more differences between them, so if you read any online comparison written prior to 2012, it's outdated.

In the remainder of this chapter, I'm going to talk about how to set up and customize both Hootsuite and TweetDeck. You don't need to set up both when you first start out. I recommend you take a look at both, and then pick one to try first. If you don't like it, then you can switch.

HOOTSUITE

You can sign up for Hootsuite at www.hootsuite.com.

It comes with two options—a paid version and a free version. You don't need the paid version.

Once you sign up, you'll be directed to a screen where you can add your Twitter profile. It'll ask you to connect to Twitter. Make sure the box to create a new tab is checked and that the box for following Hootsuite is unchecked.

Add Social Network   ✕

| Twitter |
| Facebook |
| Google+ |
| LinkedIn |
| foursquare |
| WordPress |
| MySpace |
| mixi |

Add Twitter Profile
To allow HootSuite access to your Twitter account, you must first give authorization from Twitter.com

Connect with Twitter

☑ Automatically create a new tab for this profile.

☐ Follow HootSuite on Twitter for updates and announcements

Submit

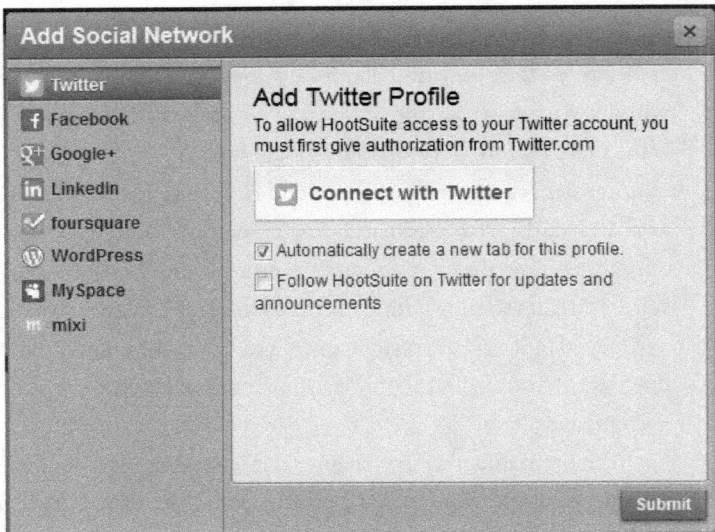

After you hit *Submit*, you'll be taken to your new tab. The default Hootsuite screen has three columns (or what they call streams) set up for you.

Home Feed is where you see tweets from everyone you've followed.

Mentions is where you see tweets from people who've included your username.

Direct Messages are private messages sent to you. Only you can see these. Everything else on Twitter is public.

Sent Tweets are, obviously, the tweets you've sent.

We'll learn more about adding and customizing columns later.

HOW TO CUSTOMIZE THE APPEARANCE OF HOOTSUITE

One of the biggest benefits of using something like Hootsuite or TweetDeck is the ability to customize them to your own liking. I'm going to walk you through the different elements that you can personalize on both Hootsuite and TweetDeck, starting with Hootsuite.

Frequency of Updates

In the top right of your Hootsuite streams, you'll see the dropdown menu I've circled below.

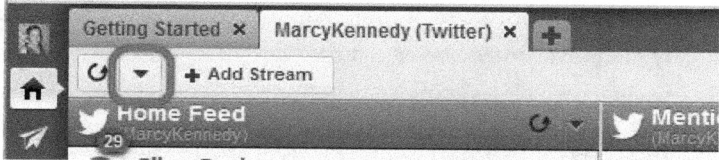

When you press it, you'll be able to choose how often Hootsuite refreshes its streams. The shortest frequency Hootsuite will refresh is two minutes. If you want to see new updates more often, you have to press **Refresh** manually by using the circular arrow to the left.

Number of Streams

You can also choose how many streams you want. You can find the sliding bar to change the number of streams on the left-hand side above your streams.

You can't change the width of your streams in Hootsuite, so the maximum number you can see at once will be determined by the size of your screen. If you have more streams than you can see at one time, you can see the ones that aren't visible by using the sliding bar at the bottom of the streams.

Optional Tip: Add your Facebook accounts as well. You shouldn't be posting from Hootsuite to Facebook, but having them at least connected helps you keep your eye on both social media accounts at once. If you see something you want to comment on, you can quickly jump over to Facebook and take care of it. It's almost as good as being in two places at once.

But can't I update Facebook from Hootsuite?

You can, but you shouldn't. Facebook is always changing the rules, but over the last little while there have been multiple problems with using outside applications to update your Facebook account. If anyone else is adding a status update using the same application at the same time, your update will be aggregated, which lumps it in a bundle where no one will see it. Also, the fact that you're updating from somewhere else is shown, meaning people know you're not actually there.

Whether or not these remain issues, it doesn't take that much longer to hop over and reply directly on Facebook.

TWEETDECK

You can sign up for TweetDeck at http://www.tweetdeck.com/.

Signing up for TweetDeck is very similar to signing up for Hootsuite.

Once you create your TweetDeck account, it will ask you to add your Twitter account.

You might receive an error message after you fill in your username and password. If you do, don't worry. Just close the error message window, and in the window that asks you to **Add Twitter Account**, click on **Add Twitter Account** again.

When the pop-up window re-opens, you'll see that you're now signed in to your Twitter account. Authorize the app.

TweetDeck is constantly changing which columns you're set up with when you first sign up. If these aren't the four you're given, don't worry. I explain all the columns later, and if some of them are missing from that list as well, Twitter has likely just renamed them. Once you're set up, you should easily be able to figure out what's what. If not, my email address is at the back of this book, and you're welcome to email me to ask.

As of spring 2014, TweetDeck sets you up with four basic columns.

Home shows you tweets from everyone you've followed. (TweetDeck sometimes changes this to call it a Timeline.)

Notifications shows you any tweets where your username has been mentioned and lists your new followers.

Messages are private messages sent to you. Only you can see these. Everything else on Twitter is public.

Activity shows you all the follow, favorite, and add-to-list actions performed by the people you follow. This column is essentially useless.

HOW TO CUSTOMIZE THE APPEARANCE OF TWEETDECK

Click the gear box in the left hand sidebar of TweetDeck. This takes you to **Settings**. (Don't confuse these with your Twitter settings. These are your TweetDeck settings.)

Once the box opens up, choose **Settings**, then **General**. This is where you'll play around with how you want TweetDeck to look.

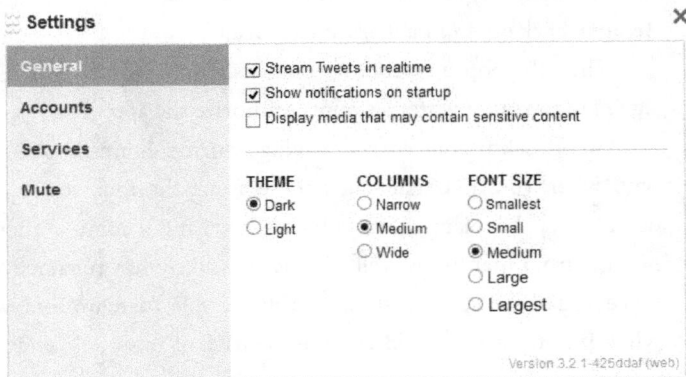

Stream Tweets in realtime is what allows TweetDeck to give you the constant updates Hootsuite doesn't.

Show notifications on startup is a completely personal preference. TweetDeck allows you to choose whether you want pop-up notifications of certain columns. When TweetDeck is shut down, those notifications won't pop-up. Instead, you can choose not to see them at all, or to see them back to back when you first start TweetDeck. I keep this box checked because I like to be caught up when I first sign in.

You have the option to choose whether you want a dark background (with white text) or a light background (with dark text). I find the dark background is easier on my eyes, but I love that TweetDeck allows you to pick what's best for you.

Choose your column size and font size, and you're set.

PART TWO

Continuing Strong

CHAPTER EIGHT

How to Stay Safe on Twitter

N ow that you're set up on either Hootsuite or TweetDeck, we're about to dive in to actually tweeting and spending time on Twitter. Before we do, we need to talk safety.

For all the wonderful things that technology provides us, it also comes with new risks. We need to be smart about our social media use because Twitter won't be fun and our platform building won't be sustainable if we don't know how to stay safe.

This chapter is all what steps you can take to protect yourself and your information online.

CHANGE YOUR PASSWORDS REGULARLY AND PROTECT THEM FROM SCAM ARTISTS

You always need to remember that Twitter is like any other site with a password. Your password needs to be strong. (Twitter tells you if you have a strong or weak password when you first sign up.) If in doubt, create a password that's at least 10 characters long and includes a number. Not all sites are case-sensitive, but for those that are, you'll also want to include at least one uppercase letter. Twitter is case-sensitive, so I encourage you to include both upper and low-ercase letters in your password. The strongest passwords will also include special characters, such as ! or @.

You also need to change your password frequently. You might not know if your account has been hacked, so by changing your password frequently, you basically wipe the slate clean. At a mini-mum, change your password every month.

Don't use a password that you're using anywhere else. If your Twitter account or your email gets hacked, you don't want a hacker going over to your website to try the same password and finding out it works, or vice-versa. Every site you use will be more secure by keeping passwords unique.

If all this talk about changing passwords and using unique pass-words has you worried that you'll forget your passwords, here are a couple tricks you can use.

Pick a quirky phrase that will be difficult to forget.

Nine giant elephants ate my prize-winning tulips.

Then turn it into an alphanumeric code.

9Ge8mpw2lips

Another option is to write you passwords down on a piece of paper and tape them to the back of a picture on your office wall (or the wall of whatever room you regularly work in). It's not a perfect solution, but if someone breaks into your house, they're probably not going to go removing pictures from your walls on the off chance that they might find your password for Twitter.

Some computer security programs (like Norton) now also offer the option to save your passwords for you. You usually only have to remember a single password to unlock this feature of the program, which then stores all the other passwords for you.

When it comes to keeping your Twitter password safe, one key thing to remember is that Twitter will *never* contact you to ask you to send them your password via email, direct message, or @ reply. If someone contacts you, claiming to be Twitter and wanting your password in this way, they're a scammer.

Here is Twitter's official policy:

> If we suspect your account has been phished or hacked, we may reset your password to prevent the hacker from misusing your account. In this case, we'll email you a link to where you can reset your password. Again, this link will always be on the *http://twitter.com/* website, and we will never ask you to provide your password via email, direct message, or @reply.

In other words, they'll send you to Twitter.com to reset your password. They will not request that you email it or send it via any other means.

WHEN YOU LOG IN, PAY ATTENTION

Most of us are super busy and log into accounts on autopilot, but this actually puts us at risk. When you sign in, make sure you're paying attention.

If you're trying to log in to Twitter.com directly, check that you're on their page. The simplest way to do this is to type www.twitter.com directly into your browser rather than allowing some secondary service to supposedly take you there, but Twitter has a good explanation of an easy way to check whether you're actually on twitter.com before giving them your log in information.

Twitter domains will always have the *http://twitter.com/* as the base domain. Here are some examples of Twitter log-in pages:
- *https://twitter.com/*
- *https://twitter.com/login*

Phishing websites will often look just like Twitter's log-in page, but will actually be a website that is not Twitter. Here are some examples of URLs that are **NOT** Twitter pages:
- *http://twitter.example.com*
- *http://twitter.photobucket.example.com*
- *http://twitter.com@example.com*

Notice how in the legitimate sites, nothing separates *Twitter* from *.com*.

In the fake sites, *Twitter* and the actual *.com* of the address are separated. They're not together as the base domain. In the third example (a particularly tricky one), there are two *.com* sections. Only the final one counts. Since the word *Twitter* isn't next to it, this is a fake site.

For TweetDeck and Hootsuite users, if you ever receive a pop-up message or any other communication claiming to be from

TweetDeck or Hootsuite and saying your account will be suspended unless you verify your password, this is also a scam. Close the program and open it again to see what happens.

Here's an example Kristen Lamb gave in her excellent post "Staying Safe in the Digital World—Digital Sheep Get Sheared and Slaughtered."

> I have also had a pop up appear when I went to get on Tweet Deck. The pop up from "Tweet Deck Security" was there to inform me that my account had been suspended for suspicious spamming activity, but that they were sure it was all a misunderstanding. If I just typed in my password, they would make sure everything was sorted and my account would be unlocked.
>
> I closed the window, logged out and logged back in. My account was fine. This was an attack.

I highly recommend that you read all of Kristen's post because it contains a lot of good tips for online safety in general, no matter what social media, email program, etc. we're using.

DON'T CLICK LINKS IN A DIRECT MESSAGE

One of the most common ways hackers get access to your Twitter account is through links in a direct message. You receive a message that says something like "Look at these funny pictures of you" or "Someone is saying really bad things about you" and they include a link. Your natural inclination is to click that link, but don't. Once you click, you give them access to your account, and they'll be using your account to send out these messages to other people.

Don't click links in a DM even if you know the person the DM is from. If their account has been hacked, the message isn't from them.

I handle all DMs with a link by deleting them. If you think the link might really lead to something you want to see, ask the person who supposedly sent it if it really came from them.

CONTACT ANYONE WHO MAY HAVE BEEN HACKED

If you get a direct message from someone and you suspect they didn't send it, contact them to tell them their Twitter account might have been hacked, and suggest that they change their password.

Unless you let the person who's been hacked know, they'll have no idea that someone has taken over their account and is using it to send out DMs with sketchy links in them.

Part of protecting our accounts is being global citizens who help other people protect theirs.

REPORT—AND BLOCK—BAD ACCOUNTS

I'm giving you this instruction with caution because not everyone understands what they should be reporting and what they shouldn't.

Reporting is serious business and can get someone's account suspended or deleted. Innocent people have had this happen to them because someone thought that just because they didn't like what was tweeted, they should report it. Or people have been reported as spam because their accounts were hacked. Do not report someone if you suspect their account has been hacked. Instead, let them know so they can change their password and free their account from the hacker.

Here is how Twitter defines spam:

Here are some common tactics that spam accounts often use:

- Posting harmful links (including links to phishing or malware sites)
- Aggressive following behavior (mass following and mass un-following for attention)
- Abusing the @reply or @mention function to post unwanted messages to users
- Creating multiple accounts (either manually or using automated tools)
- Posting repeatedly to trending topics to try to grab attention
- Repeatedly posting duplicate updates
- Posting links with unrelated tweets

Some of these are self-explanatory, but I think some of them need to be elaborated on.

Abusing the @reply or @mention function to post unwanted messages to users.

This is when someone uses @username to repeatedly send you a sales link, a link to a porn site, or to harass you in any way. #FF or other group messages don't fall into this category, and you should not report someone for mentioning you along with a block of other people unless they're doing it in a harmful manner.

Repeatedly posting duplicate updates.

This does not mean that someone posted a link to their blog two, three, or even five times. This is talking about someone who posts the same handful of tweets over and over again. You can easily tell these people if you scroll down their Twitter stream. It's repetitive and you don't see any variety or genuine interaction.

Posting links with unrelated tweets.

This is when someone writes an innocent-looking tweet and then links to a harmful site. It can also be when someone writes something unrelated to get people's interest and then links to their sales page. (It's like false advertising of a product.)

When you report someone as spam, they're also blocked from seeing your tweets and you won't see their tweets anymore.

Twitter has really cracked down on spam accounts so you don't see the above spamming techniques happening as much anymore.

If you don't want someone seeing your tweets, Twitter gives you the option to block this person. I've done this to someone who was randomly retweeting my tweets. In other words, they simply went to my Twitter stream and retweeted the first five tweets one after the other. One of those tweets was a thank you to someone who'd retweeted for me. Another was part of a conversation I was having with someone and made no sense out of context (i.e., there was no reason to RT it). I checked out the account of this person, and they seemed to be real-ish, and so I didn't want to report them. After all, they hadn't really done anything wrong. After the second time they did this massive blast of RTs, I blocked them.

When it comes to reporting people, first ask whether there could be an innocent explanation for their behavior. Only report people who are willfully spamming or engaging in other harmful behaviors.

CHECK YOUR TWITTER APPS PAGE REGULARLY

This is a housecleaning measure. About once a month or so, go to the part of your profile where all the apps you've given access to your account are listed.

Delete any you don't recognize or aren't using anymore.

DON'T TWEET ABOUT WHERE YOU'RE GOING OR WHEN YOU'LL BE AWAY FROM HOME

It's sad that this is the case, but in our world now, you can't always trust that people are who they say they are. More than that, all your tweets are public. People don't even have to be following you to see what you're tweeting.

We talked about why you shouldn't give out your address when we talked about our profiles, but there's something else you need to be aware of if you plan to tweet pictures.

Some camera phones embed location information into the metadata of your pictures. It's called geotagging, and anyone who wants to can easily figure out where you live or where you are at that moment. *The New York Times* ran an excellent article about this called "Web Photos That Reveal Secrets, Like Where You Live" that I'd encourage you to read if you plan to share any photos online.

You can turn off the geotagging feature on your smart phone (the NYT article above provides many helpful resources on how to do this), or you can strip geotag information from pictures you've already taken on your phone using apps such as deGeo (iPhone) or Photo Privacy Editor (Android).

Both Facebook and Twitter say they will now be removing location information from photos, but you shouldn't trust a social media site to do it for you because their policies are constantly changing. Be safe and do it yourself.

As I close off this chapter, I want to share a link to a TED Talk given by Del Harvey, head of Twitter's Trust and Safety Team. It's a good peek into what Twitter is actively doing to keep their users safe. You can find her TED Talk by searching for "Del Harvey: The Strangeness of Scale at Twitter" on YouTube.

CHAPTER NINE

Building Columns and Using Them to Find Readers

An application like TweetDeck or Hootsuite is only useful if you know how to customize it. We're going to focus on columns/streams and lists over this chapter and the next.

First, I'll walk you through how to set up columns on TweetDeck, then Hootsuite, and then we'll talk about what types of columns you'll want. You obviously don't need to read the material on the app you don't plan to use. (For example, if you plan to use TweetDeck, simply skip the part on Hootsuite.)

HOW TO ADD AND MOVE COLUMNS ON TWEETDECK

Open TweetDeck and you'll see **Add Column** toward the top left side. If your menu is only showing symbols, look for the + sign.

A box will open. Click on **Search**.

The new search box that opens from there will allow you to search by hashtag or by term. (We're going to talk about hashtags more in a later chapter, so don't worry too much about this for now.)

When I type in #MyWANA and hit *Enter*, TweetDeck will show me a preview of that column. Before adding any hashtag or search term as a column, you should scroll through the preview to make sure it's worth the space in TweetDeck. Not every term you search for will yield helpful results and not every hashtag is active.

TweetDeck now shows *Content*, *Users*, and *Engagement* options at the top. Ignore these unless you're looking for a specific tweet by a specific person. Otherwise, it's just static.

If you like what you see, hit *Add Column.*

The new column will automatically be added to the farthest right position, but if it's one you plan to use often, you'll want to give it a place in the first four columns.

At the top right of the newly added column, you'll see a strange little symbol that looks like this:

Click it. (This used to be an upside-down triangle, so don't be surprised if TweetDeck changes the symbol again.)

You'll now be shown options for customizing your column.

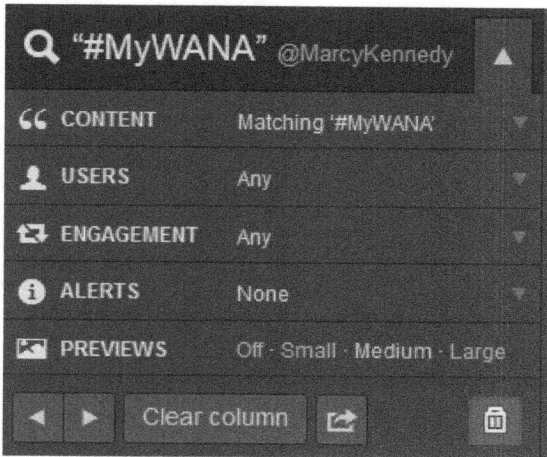

This customization is important for every column you add. One of the complaints I hear most often about TweetDeck is that people can't stand the constant interruption of TweetDeck beeping at them or flashing pop-ups on their screen. The great thing about the newest version of TweetDeck is you will only hear a notification or see a pop-up if you tell it to.

How you set these is up to your personal preferences. I'll tell you my opinion.

The **Content**, **Users**, and **Engagement** options allow you to go a little crazy. For most columns, this is a waste of time. However, if you want to search a particular column (e.g., #indiepub) for tweets pertaining to a specific topic (e.g., formatting ebooks), this is how you could do that. Otherwise, you're better off ignoring them.

I usually keep the alerts off, but you can enable a sound to notify you every time there's a new tweet in that column. (Be careful. This can get annoying fast.)

Previews allows you to decide whether you want to see a thumbnail in your columns of pictures and other media people share. I leave this on because it helps me quickly decide if I want to click on something to see a bigger version or not. I've shown you in a screen-shot below what it looks like.

The left and right arrows allow you to move the column to the left or right so that you can order your columns however suits you best.

The *Share* feature allows you to create a widget to embed that particular column in your blog. In other words, if you click that, it will take you to a spot where you can create an HTML code that will allow you to add that column to your website. If just reading about that makes your head want to explode, don't worry about it. In my humble opinion, you shouldn't be cluttering up your blog/website sidebar with a feed from a Twitter column anyway. I'll talk about a couple exceptions to this later.

The *Clear* feature allows you to erase what's in the column so that you know you're looking at fresh tweets from that point on. With a busy column like #MyWANA, I wouldn't bother doing this. In a quieter column, it's sometimes helpful because you can see at a glance if there's anything new to reply to.

WHAT DO THE OTHER BOXES IN THE TWEETDECK COLUMNS TAB MEAN?

TweetDeck frequently changes the options they offer for columns, so I'm going to cover the ones that have stayed fairly consistent over the years.

The **Home** button will allow you to add the Home column again if you delete it. The Home column includes every person you follow on Twitter. By the time you're following 1,000 or more people, it's virtually useless. It starts to move too fast to read the tweets, let alone respond to them.

The **Notifications** button will create a column featuring the people who've recently followed you or @ messaged you and also shows when you've been added to a list, retweeted, or favorited. It's basically the **Mentions** column on steroids. I love this column because of how it makes conversations easier.

The unique benefit this column adds is in the silhouette of a person with a drop down menu next to each person.

When you click that, it gives you options for interacting with those people, including tweeting them, following them, sending them a direct message, adding or removing them from lists, muting them in TweetDeck, blocking them, and reporting them.

This column is an absolutely great way to do whatever you need to. You can do this in other ways, but the Notifications column allows you to streamline the process. In my option, this is a better column to use than the @ Mentions column below.

@ Mentions is where you see tweets from people who've included your username.

You might remember the Activity column. It gives you a real-time feed of all the follow, favorite, and add-to-list actions performed by the people you follow. You could use this to find other people you might be interested in following and to see what people consider the best tweets, but in my opinion, this column is a complete waste of time. There are more efficient ways to use Twitter and make connections than to constantly be watching this column in the hopes of finding something worthwhile.

Favorites creates a column where you can see the tweets you save. To save a tweet, all you have to do is click on the star icon at the bottom of it.

Lists are the next button, but stay tuned. We'll discuss them in detail in the next chapter.

The *Scheduled* button will show you any tweets you've scheduled and allow you to get rid of them.

We already looked at how you can use *Search* to look for hashtags or terms to follow in a column. I've also used it to find people if the *Follow Me on Twitter* link on their site wasn't working.

When you type in your search term, the same box will pop up as if you'd gone through the *Add Column* button.

You can also quickly access the search feature from the top of the left-side menu bar.

Followers is exactly what it sounds like. If you click on it, it gives you a list of people who've followed you, along with their bios and a dropdown menu where you can follow them back, block them, etc.

Messages will create a column for your direct messages (the private messages). If you have Twitter email these to you, you don't need to turn this into a column.

The *User* button allows you to see what you've tweeted. Keeping an eye on this column is a really great way to make sure you're balancing your tweets between conversation, promoting others through links and retweets, and promoting your own work. In the past, this column was called Tweets.

When you click on *Trending*, it will give you a list of topics that are trending worldwide. Click on any of those terms to see a preview of what that column would have in it. I never bother with these. Personal preference. It's not why I'm on Twitter.

HOW TO ADD AND MOVE COLUMNS ON HOOTSUITE

Hootsuite gives you two options for adding a stream (their word for columns).

In the top left corner, you can click *Add Stream*.

That will bring up a box like the one below.

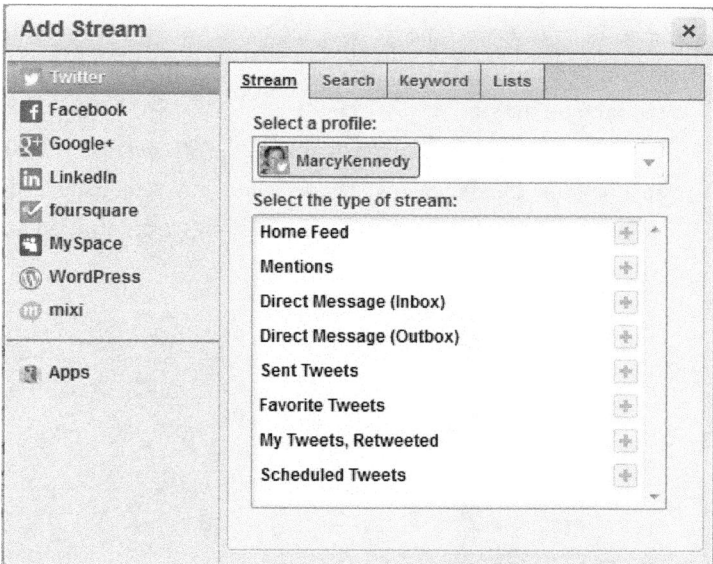

If you click the menu, you can select some of the most common streams you might want to add. By now most of them should be clear, but just in case, here's a refresher of the ones that might not be immediately obvious.

The **Home Feed** option will allow you to add the Home Feed column again if you delete it. The Home Feed column includes every person you follow on Twitter. By the time you're following 1,000 or more people, it's virtually useless. It starts to move too fast to read the tweets, let alone respond to them.

Mentions is where you see tweets from people who've included your username.

Direct Messages will create a column for your sent or received direct messages (the private messages). If you have Twitter email these to you, you don't need to turn this into a column.

Favorites creates a column where you can see the tweets you save. To save a tweet, hover over the tweet you're interested in saving. When the symbols appear, click on the upside-down triangle, and then on the star.

If you click on the **Search** tab next to the **Stream** tab, it will bring up a box like the one below. This is where you can create a column based on a hashtag. (We'll talk about hashtags more in a later chapter.)

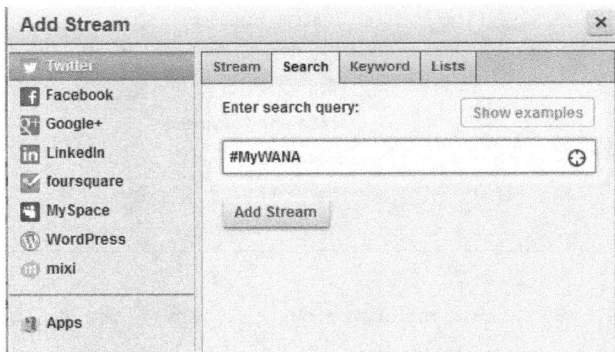

You'll notice that you don't get a preview of the stream to help you decide whether to add it. Before adding any hashtag or search term as a stream, you should scroll through a preview to make sure it's worth the space. Not every term you search for will yield helpful results and not every hashtag is active.

Because of this, if you want to add a stream based on a hashtag in Hootsuite, it's better to use the magnifying glass icon found in the top right-hand corner of your main screen. By entering the hashtag you're interested in and pressing *Enter*, you'll be able to preview it before deciding whether to add it or not.

This magnifying glass is also where Hootsuite will show you what's trending on Twitter.

The next feature in Hootsuite's Stream box is **Keywords**. This is an interesting feature unique to Hootsuite. Say you're a science fiction and fantasy writer and so you want to monitor those two terms together in one stream.

You add them each separately and then create a stream. Again, you can't preview it before adding it, but it's still a neat feature.

Hootsuite has a drag-and-drop interface for moving streams. If you hover your cursor over the title box at the top of a stream, your cursor will turn into a four-way arrow and you can just click and drag the stream to whatever location you want.

You can also set Hootsuite to give you pop-up notifications and sounds. Go back to your *Settings* and click on *Notifications*.

You can enable the notifications you'd like to receive.

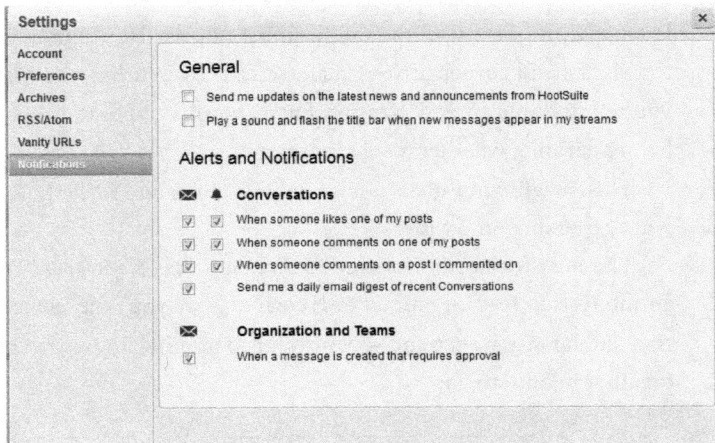

The drawback of Hootsuite over TweetDeck in this area is that Hootsuite is all or nothing. You can't choose to receive notifications for only one stream.

HOW TO USE COLUMNS TO HELP YOU FIND NON-WRITER FRIENDS

You need to connect to other writers on Twitter.

As you might have already figured out, writers are also avid readers. People who write in your genre or write about your topic probably also read in your genre or read about your topic. They're the ones who rave about books, badger their friends and family to read them, and who everyone goes to for recommendations. They're also the ones who will be your professional support network.

So don't worry if you connect mostly to writers at first. That's normal and helpful. But eventually you're going to want to branch out into making non-writer friends, and columns will help you do that, too.

We're going to look at this more when we get to the chapter on how to identify hashtags (the # sign) your potential readers might congregate around, but for now, here's the general idea.

Think about the genre you write and quickly brainstorm 10–20 words (or short phrases) that people who read your genre might also be interested in.

For example, if you write women's fiction, your list might include *fashion, cute shoes, romance, dating, motherhood,* etc.

You can also search for themes in your current book—for example, if your main character has an autistic son, a keyword might be *autism.*

Take those words, add a hashtag in front, and do a search for them as if you were going to create a column. (Remember that if you search for a phrase as a hashtag, you need to make it one word—e.g., #cuteshoes **not** #cute shoes.)

If you see what looks like active conversation happening around that term, turn it into a column so that you can follow it. Join in. Form authentic relationships.

A lot of the time, the people you talk to will add you. That's how you start to branch out.

I recommend that you only do these searches for hashtags rather than for the keywords without the hashtag sign. As we'll talk about in the chapter on hashtags, people using the hashtags expect that other people will see their tweets and might reply.

If you search for a term without a hashtag and add it to a column, this will show you every time that word is used in a tweet (even when it doesn't have a hashtag attached). Replying to one of these tweets can sometimes feel random and strange to the person who tweeted it. If they're not as well versed in Twitter, they may not have realized that a tweet without a hashtag could still be seen by non-followers. It's never a good start to come off as a stalker or eavesdropper, so stick with hashtags to be on the safe side.

CHAPTER TEN

Creating and Using Lists

One of the common complaints about Twitter is that it moves too fast and you don't know what to pay attention to. It's a valid complaint, but there's a simple solution—Twitter lists.

Lists on Twitter are just what they sound like. A Twitter list can be added to a column in TweetDeck or a stream in Hootsuite so that you're able to watch only the tweets made by the people on that list.

You can create your own lists or subscribe to lists created by others. Twitter allows you to have up to 20 lists, with 500 people per list.

However, it's important to remember that, unlike on Google+ or Facebook, where you can confine a message to a particular circle or list, on Twitter, lists only work in one direction. While you can see all the tweets of the people on your list in a single column, you can't direct a tweet only to people on a given list. Your tweets go out to everyone who follows you.

Your lists are linked to your Twitter account. They'll follow you if you switch from TweetDeck to Hootsuite or vice versa.

CREATING LISTS ON TWITTER.COM

Hit the *Me* button from the top menu bar. This will take you to your profile page. Click on *More* from beside where it gives you the number of tweets you've sent, people following you, and people you follow. That will bring up a drop-down menu with the option of looking at your lists. You can create a new list from this page.

Everything else about creating this list is the same as if you created it on TweetDeck, so keep reading!

CREATING LISTS ON TWEETDECK

Hit the *List* button in the left-hand menu bar.

It's easiest to have a list created and set up before you start trying to add people.

Account	MarcyKennedy ▼
Name	
Description	
Privacy	⦿ Public ○ Private

Give your list a name of 25 characters or less. Your list name can't start with a number.

You don't need to add a description, but you can if you want to. Your description just needs to remain under 100 characters.

As you'd imagine, public lists can be seen by anyone on Twitter. Private lists can be seen only by you. For example, perhaps you don't want people knowing who's on your list of favorite tweeters. You can make that list private.

TweetDeck gives you multiple ways to add people to lists.

If you click on someone's name, this box will pop up and then you can click the drop-down menu by the silhouette of a person.

An easier way, though, is to hover over the tweet from a person you want to add, and when the symbols appear, click on the three dots.

You can also add people directly from your Notifications column (if you created one).

You remove people by doing the same thing in reverse.

You can create a column for any of your lists by clicking the *Lists* button we saw earlier in the *Add Column* box.

CREATING LISTS ON HOOTSUITE

Lists in Hootsuite take a couple extra steps compared to creating a list in TweetDeck. Before you can add someone to a list, you first need to have that list open in a stream or it won't show up as an option when you try to add someone.

To fix this, click on *Add Stream* and then go to the *List* tab.

Select your Twitter profile.

You can now choose to either create a stream based on an existing list or create a new list the exact same way you would in TweetDeck. Add the list in question to a stream. You can now add someone to that list.

To add people to a list in Hootsuite, click on their name in one of your streams. The **Add to List** button is at the bottom of the box that pops up. Depending on the size of your screen, you may have to drag the **Bio** box up to see it.

WHEN SHOULD YOU START CREATING LISTS?

Immediately!

It might not seem like a big deal to have everyone in your Home column/stream now and to just depend on that, but believe me, the more people you follow, the more useless that column becomes. Pretty soon that column will be moving so quickly you won't be able to keep up and you'll miss great opportunities to chat with people.

This is my single biggest regret about how I came to Twitter. I didn't know about lists when I first started on Twitter, and by the time I figured out I could create them, I already had over 2,000 people. I still don't have everyone placed into lists the way I'd like.

If you start making lists when you have a small number of followers, it'll be easy to add them as you follow them.

WHAT CAN YOU DO WITH LISTS?

Make connections with agents, editors, or book reviewers.

The great part about Twitter is that people who are usually behind stone walls and inaccessible to the newbie writer are available on Twitter.

If you hope to traditionally publish, create a list for agents and editors. Not only do these people often offer links to great information, but you can also get an idea of their personality and whether they'd be a good match for you and your book. Do they sound like someone you'd like to work with? Are they kind to others? Do they keep up on new trends? What types of books do they represent and read?

Moreover, some agents will engage with their followers, asking questions and answering them. Along with commenting on their blog (if they have one), retweeting their tweets can be a way to help them become familiar with your name.

For example, for a long time, agent Sara Megibow hosted #10queriesin10tweets. She'd take the next 10 queries in her pile, and explain why she rejected them or asked for more. If you were planning to query Sara, this would be invaluable information. (It was actually a good look behind the curtain even if you didn't plan to query Sara.)

Whatever publishing path you plan on following, create a list for book reviewers. By retweeting material for them and replying to comments they make, you can start to build friendships with them. When you later send them a polite email asking if they'd be willing to read and review your book, they're more likely to accept because they already recognize your name. You've given to them first.

It also lets you know if they'd enjoy your type of book. Sending a book to someone who doesn't enjoy what you write is a waste of their time and yours, and can more easily result in a poor review.

And here's a trick a lot of people don't know—*you don't have to be following someone to add them to a list.* In other words, all those industry pros you're dying to follow but haven't because I told you not to or you'd risk skewing your social proof numbers...well, you can get all they have to offer without following them!

Unfortunately, this works in reverse, too. Say you follow someone, add them to a list, and then later decide you don't want to follow them anymore. You have to both unfollow them *and* remove them from your lists or you'll keep seeing their tweets even after you've unfollowed them.

Build relationships with other writers in your genre.

From the start, if you know what genre you're going to write in, you should be putting together a list of people you follow who also write in your genre.

When you have a genre-specific question, these people can be a great resource.

When you need beta readers who understand your genre, these are the people to turn to.

When you have a book out and want to guest post on a blog where your potential readers already hang out, you'll already have friendships with the people who run those blogs.

When you're running behind and quickly need material to tweet that would interest your readers, these people's blogs are most likely to yield what you're looking for.

Keep track of subject matter experts.

Say you're writing a book set in Australia, but you've never been there. Create a list for people you find on Twitter who live there.

Say you're writing a book with horses in it. Create a list where you can add people who mention horses or horseback riding in their bio.

As you get to know these people and they get to know you, when you have a question that can't be answered through traditional research, you'll have someone you can ask.

Connect with writers who live in your area.

Connecting with writers who live in your area means you have friends who can turn into critique groups, who you can organize writing events with (e.g., everyone meets at the local library during NaNoWriMo and writes for two hours, you share a book signing), or who you can meet up with at local conferences.

Reciprocate for people who regularly RT your tweets.

As your follower numbers grow, it's going to be difficult to keep track of which ones are actively engaging and trying to help you by retweeting your tweets. Yet these are the people who've already taken the initiative to try to reach out to you and do something nice. If you start putting them into a list, it'll help you retweet for them in return when they tweet something great, and it'll also help you keep the conversation going.

(Just remember to retweet only good material. Your credibility is on the line if you tweet a sloppy or boring blog post.)

Stay in touch with fans that contact you about your book or say something good about your writing.

Readers like social media because it gets them a little bit closer to their favorite authors, so when you take the time to personally reply to one of their tweets to cheer them on or suggest a book by another author they might like, it builds rapport.

Some authors also provide special bonuses just for their Twitter followers, such as tweeting a link to a new short story that you don't advertise elsewhere or offering a single-day Smashwords coupon code. Even though you can't target these bonuses to one list, if you know you have a large number of fans following you, it can guide your decisions.

Don't confine yourself to the lists I've suggested here. Once you start thinking about lists, you'll find ways to customize them that fit you as an individual.

THE PUBLIC VS. PRIVATE LIST DEBATE

While it's up to you how you set your lists, I think some of them should be kept private.

Lists best kept public: Publishing industry pros, book reviewers, genre authors, authors in my area

Keep these public because others might want to subscribe to them.

Lists best kept private: Readers, RTers, favorite tweeters

Keep these private because no one needs to know who's on those lists and who isn't.

HOW LISTS SAVE YOU TIME

You're probably looking at this and wondering how you're ever going to keep up with all these lists every day.

You don't.

Let's assume you only have 5–10 minutes a day for Twitter. Choose one of the columns you created based on a list, and see if there's someone you can chat with for that time. While you're chatting with them, scan a different column for people you can RT something for.

Choose a different two lists the next day.

Rather than trying to sort through all your followers each time you get on, you now have a goal.

If you try to keep up with everyone all the time, you're just going to feel stressed. Building relationships on Twitter takes time the same way building relationships in the real world takes time.

And remember, Twitter should only be part of your social media plan. If nothing else, you should have a blog. People will follow you from Twitter to your blog, and you'll chat with them more there. Twitter and blogging complement each other in that way.

We'll look at more time saving tips in a later chapter.

IT SHOULD GO WITHOUT SAYING, BUT...

Don't target these people. Don't send each of the people on your reader list a tweet asking them to buy your new book. Don't try to pitch to agents via Twitter.

All of this is about building relationships and interacting on an authentic level. All lists do is make it easier for you to keep up with the people you're following. They're a tool for building relationships, not a tool to collect names so you can spam them later.

Be a real person and, when the time comes, people will want to help you. You won't need to use any marketing techniques that will leave you feeling slimy.

CHAPTER ELEVEN

Link Shorteners

One of my first Twitter students called the strange, short links you see on Twitter "alien links" and I loved it so much that I expect I'll be calling them that from now on.

As you've probably noticed by now, one of the challenges of Twitter is fitting everything into the 140 characters. Those "alien links" can be life savers because they take something that looks like this...

http://www.marcykennedy.com/do-you-like-to-have-the-last-word-the-story-of-echo/

and turn it into this...

bit.ly/S83Hh1

In terms of numbers, it reduced 80 characters down to 13.

So the first thing I want to do is show you some of your options for shortening your links, and then we'll look at how they can actually help you connect with people. I'm taking so much time on link shorteners because they have many valuable applications for authors beyond Twitter, as well as on Twitter.

GOOGLE URL SHORTENER

http://goo.gl/

If you've heard of Triberr, this is the link shortener used by Triberr.

If you paste a long link into Goo.gl, this is what you'll get.

It pulls in a little image of the page on the right so that you can be sure that's the page you were meaning to link to, and above that image is the shortened link.

If you were to click on ***Details***, you'll see what I think it the coolest feature of Goo.gl: They create a QR code for the page.

If you were to take a scan of this with your smart phone, it should take you directly to my post.

Knowing where and how to easily create a QR code is a valuable tool. Many authors are including QR codes on the back of their books to take readers to their website/blogs. They're including QR codes on their business cards or book swag to take people to their websites, pages where they can buy their books, or special giveaways.

For Goo.gl links, if you add a + sign to the end of the shortened URL, it gives you great stats on how many people have clicked your link, when they clicked it, where they're from, and what browser they're using.

The downside to Goo.gl URLs is that they're public, so anyone can see your analytics. I don't think this is a big issue, but if that idea bothers you, you've been warned.

TINYURL

http://tinyurl.com/

Typing in a long URL on their site will give you the following result.

> The following URL:
>
> **http://www.marcykennedy.com/how-much-res ponsibility-should-we-take-for-others-ac tions/**
>
> has a length of 86 characters and resulted in the following TinyURL which has a length of 26 characters:
>
> **http://tinyurl.com/96w4ztb**
> [Open in new window]
>
> Or, give your recipients confidence with a preview TinyURL:
>
> **http://preview.tinyurl.com/96w4ztb**
> [Open in new window]

TinyURLs have two advantages.

First, they offer a preview feature. Some people distrust short links because they don't know where they're being taken. The preview URL is shorter, but when someone clicks on it, they'll be able to see the full URL address and then choose whether they want to proceed to the site. However, there's a catch. For people to even trust the preview short link, they need to know what that means. Very few people will.

The other thing that makes TinyURLs special is that they allow you to customize your shortened URLs.

Say I have a long URL that's

http://www.marcykennedy.com/my-book-title-now-available-for-sale.

I could tell TinyURL that I want it to read tinyurl.com/mybooktitle and it would create that for me (as long as it was available).

The applications for this go beyond Twitter. You could create a shortened link to use on your business cards, for example.

The downside to TinyURL is that it doesn't give you any statistics on how many times your URL is clicked.

For both Goo.gl and TinyURL, you can create a short URL and take it back to whatever program you're using to tweet. Unfortunately, that's not very time effective.

Which brings us to the two URL shorteners built into Hootsuite and TweetDeck.

OW.LY

http://ow.ly/url/shorten-url

This is the default link shortener used by Hootsuite.

The major drawback to Ow.ly is that, if you use it direct from their site, it requires you to verify that you're a human and not a malicious program. In the past, they used a Captcha, which are universally hated. Now they make you play a little "game." (The last time I checked, you had to move two bouncing sheep into a sleeping man's dream bubble.)

If you use it through Hootsuite, no verification is required.

Ow.ly also doesn't give you stats on clicks, etc. This is really disappointing because you don't have any way to easily track what's happening with your tweets. I'm hoping Hootsuite and Ow.ly get their act together in the future to fix this.

Shortening a link on Hootsuite is easy.

Click in the *Compose* box at the top left of the screen and this box will open. Type your message. Then paste your link in the link box, click *Shrink*, and Hootsuite places it in your message.

BIT.LY

https://bitly.com/

I've saved this one for last because it's the best.

Bit.ly recently expanded to let users use them as a kind of bookmarking site as well. You can get an app for your browser so that, when you find a page you like, you Bitmark it. Bit.ly also lets you make stats private if you want.

Just like with the others, if you want to manually create a bit.ly link, you simply copy and paste. Recently, bit.ly introduced the option to customize your shortened link the same way you can using TinyURL.

But what's especially good about bit.ly links is the analytics they provide.

The screen shot above is what I got when I copied the Bit.ly link Janice Hardy tweeted of this post. I pasted it into my browser and simply added the + sign.

Bit.ly tells me how many people saved this link, how many people shared it, and how many clicks it received.

Along the bottom of the image, I want you to notice a couple things. To the left of the short link I can copy is what looks like a little blue squiggly box. If I click on that, it gives me a QR code for this post, just like Google's link shortener would have.

You can also see how I can choose to look at either how many people clicked specifically on the Bit.ly link shared by Janice **or** I can get global stats (which tells me about everyone who's interacting with this link).

If I scroll down the page, I can see all kinds of stats about when people clicked the link.

30 clicks on this bitmark

16 Clicks
Oct 25, 2012

Total
Past 30 Days
Past 14 Days
Past 7 Days
Past 24 Hours
Past Hour

10

0 Oct 22, 2012   Oct 23, 2012   Oct 24, 2012   Oct 25, 2012   Oct 26, 2012   Oct 27, 2012   Oct 28, 2012

All times are in UTC-4

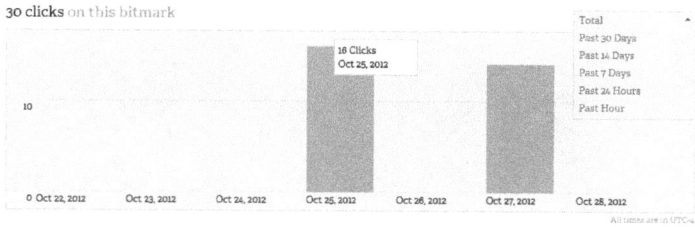

It'll also show me what people are using to click Twitter/TweetDeck or Hootsuite, as well as what countries they're in.

Referrers

hootsui.
13%

twitter.
87%

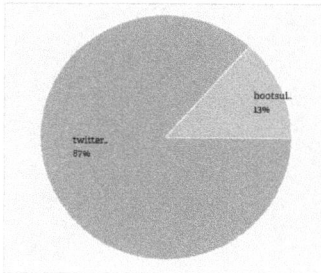

Locations: 5 Countries

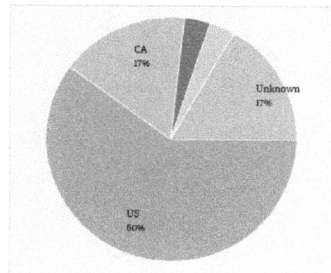

CA
17%

Unknown
17%

US
60%

These aren't just useless stats. If you realize you have a growing readership from Australia or the UK, when you have a book for sale, you're going to want to make sure it appears on online sites that people in those countries can purchase from. If you don't, you're missing out on potential sales to these people who already like you and like your voice.

But here's what I like best about Bit.ly for connecting with people.

TWEETS

Is Genre Dying? goo.gl/XuLmQ via @MarcyKennedy

about 2 hours ago

Is Genre Dying? - by Marcy Kennedy | Marcy Kennedy
ow.ly/ePF4h

about 2 hours ago

RT @MarcyKennedy: Is Genre Dying?
marcykennedy.com/is-genre-dying/

1 day ago

Is Genre Dying? marcykennedy.com/is-genre-dying/

1 day ago

Writing high-impact stories "will take...the courage to
not settle for writing books that are good enough."

This is a cropped picture, but if I could show you the whole list, you'd see that it shows me everyone who tweeted my post.

I pasted the image above because I wanted you to be able to see something specific. If you check out the links, you'll see it doesn't just show me people who used Bit.ly short links, either. There's an Ow.ly link in there, a Goo.gl link, and even a horrible long link from my website when my link shortener was broken.

Also notice that I'm not tagged in all these tweets, so unless I checked Bit.ly, I'd never know that these people were enjoying my posts. Now that I know, I can thank them, RT for them, follow them if I'm not already, or start a conversation with them. If I click on their picture, I'm taken directly to their Twitter profiles.

While you do want to always try to reach new people, the most important people to connect with are the ones who already show some interest in what you're writing. These are the people who are most likely to become your true fans.

CONNECTING TWEETDECK TO BIT.LY

If you're on TweetDeck, you need to manually connect TweetDeck to Bit.ly. It's easy to do, and once you have them linked, you paste the long URL directly into the **Compose Tweet** box on TweetDeck, and TweetDeck shortens the link when you post. You don't need to do anything to shorten it.

The first thing you'll need to do is create a Bit.ly account. It's free, and it doesn't take long.

Then, while signed in, go to http://bitly.com/a/your_api_key

(There are underscores between *your* and *api* and between *api* and *key*. Remember, you must be signed in to Bit.ly already when you use that link!)

Keep that page open, and open TweetDeck.

In the left-hand menu, open your **Settings**.

Go to the **Services** tab and enter the information it asks for.

Application Settings		✕
General	Link Shortening	Bit.ly ▾
Accounts	Bit.ly Username	
Services	Bit.ly API Key	
Global Filter		

Save, and you're done.

HOW LINK SHORTENERS HELP PEOPLE TWEET YOUR POSTS

Part of what you should want to do is encourage people to tweet your blog posts. After all, Twitter can be a great traffic driver.

This means that you also want to connect a link shortener to your blog if you can.

If you're on a wordpress.com site, then your blog already comes with a link shortener. This is an image of the box that pops up from Jenny Hansen's site when you hit the Twitter button.

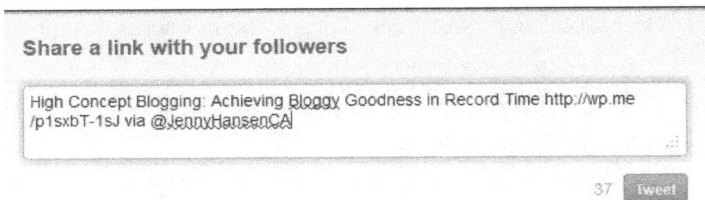

Share a link with your followers

High Concept Blogging: Achieving Bloggy Goodness in Record Time http://wp.me
/p1sxbT-1sJ via @JennyHansenCA

37 Tweet

You can see that it uses the wp.me short link that's unique to Wordpress.

To find where to enable the Twitter button, log in to the back-side of your blog, click on **Settings**, then on **Sharing**. From there, it's a matter of dragging and dropping.

If you're on a wordpress.org site, which many of you will probably end up at if writing is your long-term career, you have a lot of options for sharing buttons.

Here's what you absolutely don't want it to look like when someone clicks the Tweet button on one of your posts:

Mastering Showing and Telling in Your Fiction: A Busy
Writer's Guide

http://marcykennedy.com/2014/03/mastering-showing-telling-fiction/ via @MarcyKennedy

That long link is going straight to Twitter like that. It doesn't leave room for people to add anything. In fact, it'd be over the character limit. It certainly doesn't leave room to retweet.

You want it to look like this:

Mastering Showing and Telling in Your Fiction: A Busy Writer's Guide http://wp.me/p3h9G6-1xq via @MarcyKennedy

If you're on a wordpress.org site, there are currently only two options for sharing plugins that allow you to use link shorteners.

Sharaholic, which is also called Sexy Bookmarks, allows you to choose between various link shortening services. Unfortunately, due to a conflict with Bit.ly's API key, you can't connect it to Bit.ly. Because of what I showed you before with how Bit.ly pulls in information from other short links, this isn't a big deal. If you want to use Sharaholic, I recommend connecting it to Goo.gl.

The shortener I use on my site is **Jetpack**. It's less glitchy and uses the same wp.me as you'd get on a wordpress.com site. It integrates well with all social networks. The added benefit to these is their permanence. As long as wordpress is around, the wp.me shortlinks will stay stable.

And now that you know how to make more room in your tweets, we can talk about filling that space with hashtags.

CHAPTER TWELVE

Hashtags

As you may have already noticed, when you add a # in front of a word or phrase (with no spaces between the words), that creates a hashtag that is clickable and which people can search for.

To remind you how hashtags are used, here's a little "Anatomy of a Tweet" diagram.

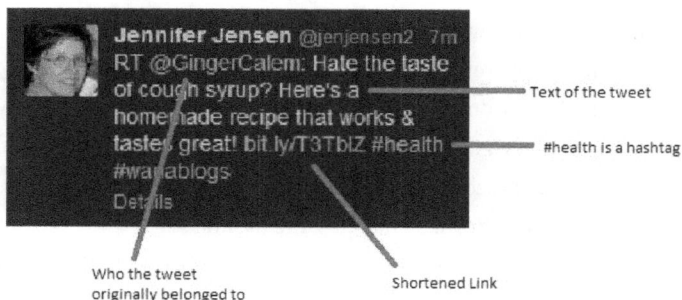

Jennifer Jensen @jenjensen2 7m
RT @GingerCalem: Hate the taste of cough syrup? Here's a homemade recipe that works & tastes great! bit.ly/T3TbIZ #health #wanablogs
Details

Text of the tweet

#health is a hashtag

Who the tweet originally belonged to

Shortened Link

When you put a hashtag at the end of your tweet, that tweet is now seen by everyone who's watching that hashtag, not just the people who follow you. Using hashtags and creating a column in TweetDeck (or a stream in Hootsuite) to follow them can introduce you to a whole new group of people you'd never have met otherwise.

But here's the catch. You can't just slap a # sign in front of any old word and expect results. Not every hashtag is actively used and watched. You have to find ones that are. If you use abandoned hashtags, you might as well have not included a hashtag at all.

Before I tell you all about how to find valuable hashtags, we need to cover some rules on proper hashtag use.

HASHTAG ETIQUETTE

Don't use a #hashtag for #every #second #word within the text of your tweet. It gets really #annoying, you #look like a #spambot, and you make it #hard to #read. It's okay to have a hashtag in your tweet, but limit it to one, and place the rest at the end.

You also don't need to use every conceivable hashtag. Choose one to three good ones, and then trust your network to change them when they retweet. That's part of working together. Moreover, if you use more than three hashtags, Twitter considers this spam and you could end up with your account suspended.

When you retweet something, make sure you change the hashtags. If you don't, you risk clogging up the column of anyone following the original hashtag. You also aren't helping out the original tweeter as much as you could be if you got their tweet in front of a fresh audience through changing the hashtag.

If you're scheduling tweets (more on the dangers of scheduling and automation in Chapter Fourteen), never schedule two tweets in a row using the same hashtags. If you're not going to be there to monitor the columns, you need to be extremely careful to spread out your hashtags so you don't unintentionally clog up a slower moving hashtag. Or better yet, don't use hashtags at all.

Don't include hashtags in the titles of your blog posts. Why? When people tweet your post from your blog or using Triberr, your title is what goes directly to Twitter. Which means...you guessed it—you clog up the column/stream of that hashtag.

BEST HASHTAGS FOR WRITERS

I can't list every useful hashtag (in part because hashtags come and go), but I can get you started with a list of the most popular hashtags for writers.

#MyWANA

The community built around this hashtag is supportive and friendly, and Kristen Lamb (originator of the hashtag) monitors it to try to keep it that way. You can read more about it (and Kristen's endorsement of the value of hashtags) in Join the Love Revolution #MyWANA.

(https://warriorwriters.wordpress.com/join-the-love-revolution-mywana/)

#amwriting/#amediting

These hashtags are just what they sound like—online water coolers for writers who are writing or editing. If you watch these columns, you'll easily find another writer to encourage or chat with.

#writetip/#writingtips

You won't find much conversation centering around either of these, but they're a good source to watch for tips and posts on craft and publishing.

#1k1hr

If you're looking for a way to increase your productivity, try the #1k1hr hashtag. The idea is to go offline for one hour to write. Your goal is to hit at least 1,000 words in that hour. By using the #1k1hr hashtag, you give others a chance to join you, and when the hour is done, you share your word counts to keep each other accountable. (**#wordcount** is another handy hashtag to add when you finish.)

Genre Hashtags

You can use these to connect if you write in one of the following genres. Some of them will host a weekly "chat" where people in that genre get together to talk on Twitter.

#SciFiChat – This chat is held Fridays from 3:00–4:00 pm Eastern. You can find more details on David A. Rozansky's (the moderator's) website.

#KidLitChat – Held on Tuesdays at 9:00 pm Eastern, you can find more details at www.kidlitchat.blogspot.ca.

#RWA (Romance Writers of America)

#ACFW (American Christian Fiction Writers)

#MGLit (Middle Grade Lit)

#SCBWI (Society of Children's Books Writers and Illustrators)

Industry Hashtags

These hashtags aren't so much for conversation as they are for distributing information.

#getpublished

#promotip

#publishing

#askagent – If you keep an eye on this hashtag, various agents will randomly drop in and take questions. Unfortunately, they don't have set times for this, but if you want to traditionally publish, it's worth at least keeping it open and reading the chats even if you can't participate.

#askeditor

#askauthor

#indiepub – This hashtag can be spammy, so I don't recommend leaving it open all the time. It's worth skimming once a week or so to see if there's anything good.

Creativity Helpers

#WritingPrompt

#StoryStarter

HASHTAGS WHERE WRITERS AND READERS OVERLAP

But of course we don't want to connect with just other writers. We also want to connect with readers. A nice way to ease into this can be to use hashtags that are specifically designed for writers and readers to connect.

#FridayReads

Every Friday, book lovers share what they're planning to read over the weekend or the book that they're reading now and love/hate.

#BookGiveaway

If you're doing a promo giveaway, this hashtag is watched by people who are eager to snatch up free reads.

HASHTAGS BY SUBJECT

As I mentioned in the chapter on columns, hashtags can be a great way to connect with potential readers. The challenge can sometimes be finding them. I've put together a sample list to help you get started. Obviously, I can't provide a list of hashtags for every conceivable genre, so I've given you this sample to help you start thinking about what hashtags might apply to your genre.

Science Hashtags

#scienceed

#scichat

#science

#physics

#scienceteacher

#scienceteachers

#technology

#sciencenews

#biology

#edchat

#math

#CERN

#climatechange

#chemistry

#edtechchat

#geology

#anatomy

#NASA

#ecosystems

#lifesciences

#teachers

#sciam

#genetics

#astronomy

#scienceblogging

#computerscience

#school

#socialscience

#nutrition

You can read about each of these hashtags at "30 Twitter Hashtags for Science Lovers" (http://www.onlinedegrees.org/30-terrific-twitter-hashtags-for-science-teachers/).

History Hashtags

Along with the more general hashtags below, you can also think about what hashtags might be associated with the particular era you're writing about.

#LightOnHistory – Launched by a historical fiction writer as a place for writers, history lovers, and historical fiction readers to connect

#sschat – Social studies chat between teachers

#socialstudies

#history

#ushistory

#civics

#historychat

Social Advocacy Hashtags

If you're writing non-fiction, or if your novel makes a statement about a particular element of our world (e.g., human trafficking, disabilities), you might be able to tap into the communities around some of these hashtags.

#socialgood

#socialchange

#cause

#causes

#volunteer

#volunteers

#volunteering

#4change

#video4change

#giveback

#dogood

#philanthropy

#charity

#charitytuesday

#nptech

#crisiscommons

#socent

#crowdfunding

#crowdsourcing

#socialbusiness

#changemakers

#BOP

#entrepreneurs

#csr

#microfinance

#socialenterprise

#sofinance

#neweconomy

#humanrights

#poverty

#hunger

#aid

#diversity

#sustainability

#health

#healthcare

#sdoh

#disabilities

#green

#eco

#earthtweet

#humantrafficking

#climate

#climatechange.

#solar

#fairtrade

Make sure you understand the use of each of these hashtags before using them. You can read more about them at "45 Hashtags for Social Change" (http://www.socialbrite.org/2011/12/27/45-hashtags-for-social-change/).

WHERE TO LOOK FOR MORE HASHTAGS

The hashtags I've shared so far in this chapter will get you started, but eventually you'll want to do your own research and find hashtags that more specifically apply to your interests and your books. There are websites that can help you do just that.

Hashtags.org

Hashtags.org gives you data that can help you find the places where people who might like your books hang out, when they're most likely to be there, and a bunch of other great tidbits.

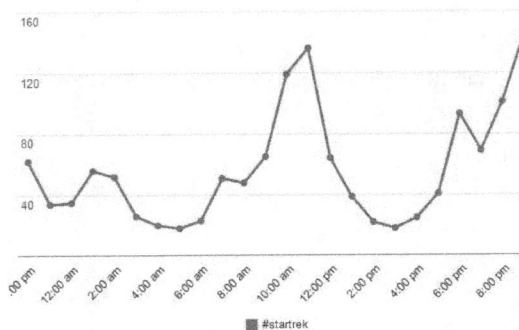

#startrek

I used the hashtag #startrek for our example. This trend graph shows you when that hashtag is most frequently used. In just a quick glance, I can see that if I want to share a tweet about Star Trek and use that hashtag, the best time is going to be between 10:00 am and 11:00 am or after 8:00 pm.

Hashtag.org also does some of the leg work for you in actually listing the people who are using this hashtag most often. This gives you people you can immediately check out on Twitter and see if you might want to follow them and interact because you already share a common interest.

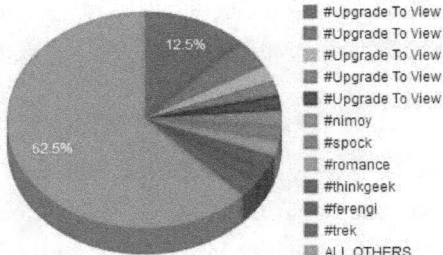

#startrek Related Hashtags

Upgrade Your Account To See Tag Names

But here's one of the best things. Hashtags.org provides suggestions for other similar hashtags that might work instead. You're never going to be able to follow every possible hashtag, so, by knowing the related hashtag, you can take a peek at them and then focus your attention on the one with the most people actively participating. Unfortunately, if you want to see the top results, you have to pay for them.

If you're pinching your pennies and don't want to pay for an upgraded account to see those top-rated related hashtags, I found a free alternative.

Tagdef.com

Tagdef.com gives you related hashtags for free. They won't rank them for you, but that's okay because you're going to look at them and pick the one that fits you best anyway. Or you could choose a few and alternate them.

As you can see in the image below, Tagdef also has a drop down menu, so if you start typing a hashtag, it gives you suggestions for how you might finish it. This is priceless if you're blanking on ideas.

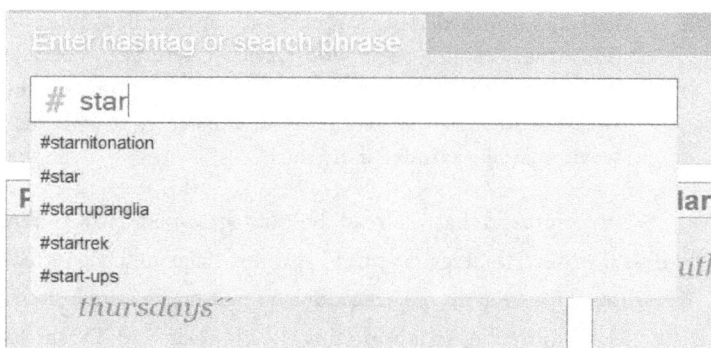

As you might imagine from the name, Tagdef.com also gives you a definition for each hashtag you search for.

Once you've found a hashtag that might work, another good site for checking whether there's a thriving community around that particular hashtag is Twubs.

Twubs

Twubs is a user-generated hashtag directory. You can look through their index (though this would take a long time since there are over 2,000 entries for M alone) or you can search for a hashtag. While Twubs does give you a live feed of tweeters currently using that hashtag, it doesn't provide you with alternatives or any of the extra information Hashtags.org does.

The real value in Twubs is that users form groups around the hashtags they like.

Here's what Sprout Social says about Twubs:

> Since the information is user-generated, you can see what hashtags are popular under categories such as books, conferences, the Internet, movies, news, politics, and much more.
>
> Since Twubs is one of the few sites where you can find hashtags grouped into categories, it's an excellent place to find other Twitter users with similar interests to connect with. Once you start interacting with other people on the site and through Twitter, you can expand your own network with like-minded individuals.

(I recommend that you read their full article on "How to Find the Best Twitter Hashtags" at http://sproutsocial.com/insights/twitter-hashtags/ for even more suggestions on hashtags research sites.)

Many of the big groups on this site are related to TV shows, but you can use that to your advantage. What TV show are the people who would enjoy your book likely to be watching? What TV shows do you love and want to talk about?

Twubs also allows you to register a hashtag into a group if there isn't already a group created. So if you want to try to build a community around a hashtag, you can register it and promote it. This is more advanced, but could have some real potential if you're able to mobilize a community.

CHAPTER THIRTEEN

What Should We Tweet About?

I've spent a lot of time in this book helping you set up your accounts so you look like a professional and teaching you how to use the available tools to make your time on Twitter easier and more effective. But in the end, what really matters is what we tweet. In the next two chapters, we're going to look at what we should tweet about and how to make those tweets great.

When it comes to deciding how to spend our time on Twitter, it's not as complicated as you think.

1/2 conversation
1/4 promotion
1/4 reciprocation

You'll find some change week by week on which you find easier. Some weeks, I have so many links I want to share that I'm heavy on reciprocation. Other weeks, I end up in a lot of great conversations and so I'm heavy on conversation. I find promotion very difficult because I don't like to talk about myself, so I have to watch that I actually share links to my content.

This isn't a rigid schedule where you have to worry if your tweets don't divide perfectly based on these categories. This is a rule of thumb meant to help us keep balance so that we can let people know what we have to offer without being spammy and so that we can form those ever-valuable relationships.

So let's break each of them down so you understand what each category contains.

CONVERSATION

A lot of people find the chatting aspect of Twitter to be the hardest part. They don't know how to start a conversation and aren't sure what the etiquette is, so I'm going to answer the questions I most commonly get about this particular element.

Can I just join an ongoing conversation?

You can. Twitter is a lot like a work water cooler where people come and go, joining in and dropping out of a conversation as they're able.

I'll give you an example. I was talking with another writer I know (@KassandraLamb). She and I are connected on Facebook and frequently talk on Twitter using #MyWANA. We'd both assumed we were already following each other on Twitter, and discovered we weren't. We were chatting about that when @AmberWest (another friend) noticed our conversation and joined us with this tweet.

> **amberwest** @amberwest   1d
> @MarcyKennedy Same thing with
> me. I think sometimes I assume
> #MyWANA peeps I talk to are in my
> follow list too. @KassandraLamb
> Details

This is really normal on Twitter. It's more than normal. It's part of the culture, and is one of the things I like about it.

You'll notice that, although Amber replied to me (my username begins the tweet), she also included Kassandra by adding her username at the end, and she kept the hashtag we were using. If you're joining a conversation, it's polite to include the usernames of the people who were already there rather than just the person whose particular tweet you're replying to.

As a general rule, if a conversation is happening on a hashtag (i.e., people are adding a hashtag to their tweets), they intend it to be seen by many people and want them to join in.

If there's no hashtag, and you feel like you might be intruding, you can say something like "Sorry to tweet jack…" and then write the rest of what you wanted to say. That's the Twitter way of saying you don't mean to rudely hijack the conversation but you'd like to join in.

Do I have to answer immediately?

I find that people have a lot of confusion about this. They think that you have to be tied to Twitter or tied to your computer to chat with people. This is absolutely false. It's smoother and more fun if you're able to talk to someone else while you're both on, but you can still have conversations even if you and the person you're tweeting to are never on at the same time.

Here's an example of a conversation I had. (This is all public on Twitter, so I'm not showing you anything private or confidential.)

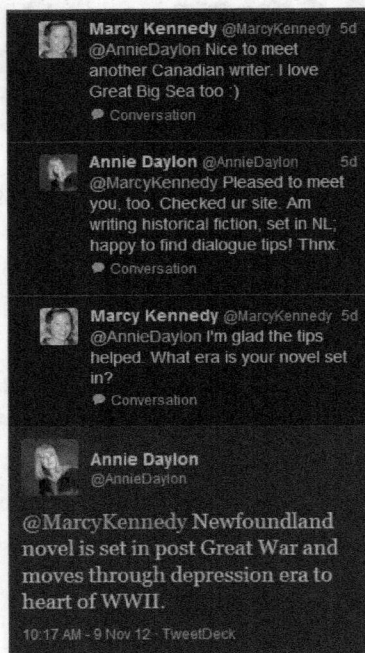

> **Marcy Kennedy** @MarcyKennedy 5d
> @AnnieDaylon Nice to meet another Canadian writer. I love Great Big Sea too :)
> 💬 Conversation
>
> **Annie Daylon** @AnnieDaylon 5d
> @MarcyKennedy Pleased to meet you, too. Checked ur site. Am writing historical fiction, set in NL; happy to find dialogue tips! Thnx
> 💬 Conversation
>
> **Marcy Kennedy** @MarcyKennedy 5d
> @AnnieDaylon I'm glad the tips helped. What era is your novel set in?
> 💬 Conversation
>
> **Annie Daylon** @AnnieDaylon
> @MarcyKennedy Newfoundland novel is set in post Great War and moves through depression era to heart of WWII.
> 10:17 AM - 9 Nov 12 - TweetDeck

This conversation started at 8:58 one evening. Annie replied at 9:17 am the next day. I wasn't on at that time, so I sent the third tweet you see above at 1:47 pm that day. As you can see, Annie replied to that one the following day. This conversation actually continued beyond this for another day as we talked about our books.

This wouldn't work on another platform like Facebook, but it's very common on Twitter.

It used to be difficult to keep up with these stretched out conversations, but TweetDeck and Hootsuite have now added a feature called *Conversation* that will show you the entirety of a conversation so you can refresh your memory.

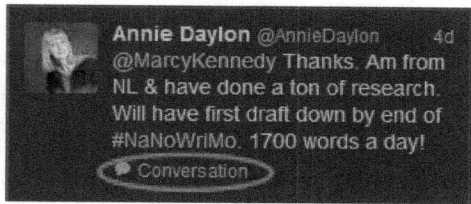

Annie Daylon @AnnieDaylon 4d
@MarcyKennedy Thanks. Am from
NL & have done a ton of research.
Will have first draft down by end of
#NaNoWriMo. 1700 words a day!
Conversation

How do I start a conversation?

Normally, if you have columns open where you're following relevant lists or hashtags, this won't be a problem. There will already be a conversation going on that you can join if you don't feel comfortable starting one yourself.

That said, if you want to take the initiative or you can't find a conversation to join, here are some ideas.

Pick one of your followers that you haven't talked to in a while and send them a tweet about something you know you have in common (or if they're a writer, you can ask how their writing is going).

Write your link tweets in a way that generates conversation. We'll talk about this more in the next chapter, but well-written tweets will often get people not only clicking the link you share and retweeting but also sending you a response on twitter.

Diane Capri @DianeCapri 1d
Are You A Jerk Without Realizing
It? goo.gl/6RZ7W via
@MarcyKennedy
Details

Karen Keller
@KarenKeller

@DianeCapri @MarcyKennedy it's
been my experience that jerks
usually know who they are!

2:23 PM · 12 Nov 12 · web

In this example, Diane tweeted my post. I'd written my title in a way that I knew would work well on Twitter because I realize that many people won't change the title before tweeting it. I got the response above, and it started a conversation.

Post something interesting, something you think people will relate to, or something topic-related (if you're adding a hashtag). The best way I can explain this is to give you a bunch of examples.

Tweet by Patrick Thunstrom:

I think tomorrow's #ROW80 post is going to be a bit of a downer. Stepping away from projects is never fun.

Tweet by Pauline Baird Jones:

A hubs should not get between a woman and her cookie dough.

Tweet by Lindsey Carmichael:

Why isn't the real world like musicals? I know my life could use some spontaneous dance numbers...

One of the funniest conversations I had on Twitter was when I asked whether people would rather eat a teaspoon of salt or a stick of butter. It was a Friday afternoon, everyone wanted the weekend to arrive, and a silly break was what we needed.

Ideally, you'll choose something you know will interest your audience.

For example, if you're writing women's fiction, you might tweet "Which do you like better – stilettos or wedges?"

If you're a fantasy writer, you might tweet "Superman vs. Batman in a throw-down. Who would win?"

I know that at first it might be difficult to see the point of the conversation portion, but this is really how we bond as individuals. People get to know us and like us, and we get to know and like them.

It's also how people know we're there and actively engaged.

PROMOTION

Promotion is the portion of twitter that's about you. Share about your book. Link to your blog. Direct people to your Facebook page.

The trick to Twitter is doing promotion right.

WRONG: Please Like My Facebook Page!

RIGHT: Post something great on your Facebook page and then link to it on Twitter. Agent Rachelle Gardner does this well, as does freelance writer Lisa Hall-Wilson.

WRONG: Buy My Book!

RIGHT: This one can be trickier because we have to make sure that these tweets are offering value to our followers.

Let me explain what I mean by that. Telling someone about our book benefits us. It doesn't necessarily benefit the person who sees our tweet or hears about our book. Instead of telling people we have a book, we need to show them what's in it for them.

For a non-fiction book, it's easy to come up with the benefits your book could provide.

For a novel, this is about entertainment. You can't convince a person they'll like your book by telling them how great it is. You have to convince them through interesting content. (And, of course, remember that all of this assumes you're also working on building relationships.)

If you have a logline, you can tweet that with a link to your book.

If you're doing a charity event, have your book on sale for a limited time, or are offering something else that might benefit your reader (or someone else), you could tweet about that.

Really, though, beyond that, the best strategy is to strategically use your blog. You see Kristen Lamb do this. She writes a post she knows will interest people who might also like her books, and at the bottom of the post, she includes a paragraph about her book. It's a very soft sell technique, and it works because she's given value before asking for anything in return.

What about tweets featuring quotes from reviewers?

If your book got a glowing review, you're likely to want to share. As long as you do this with a light hand, it's okay. Don't tweet the same review more than once, and make sure you balance this out with conversation and reciprocation.

WRONG: New Blog Post Up! Please Share!

RIGHT: We'll be talking about how to write a good tweet (including tweeting about the content of your blog posts) in the next chapter.

RECIPROCATION

Even though this element is called reciprocation, it actually has a few elements to it.

Retweet for people who've commented on your blog, who you've talked to, or who've retweeted for you (as long as they have good content).

Tweet the material of people you like even if they haven't done anything for you.

Tweet for people you want to start connecting with. Don't stop tweeting their material after one or two tries. For people who are busy, high-profile, or have a large number of followers, it can take a little while before they start to recognize your name. Beyond this, you don't know that they aren't watching even if they don't reply.

Tweet material that would interest your potential future readers. I write fantasy so I tweet about other fantasy books, about *Star Trek*, about mythology, etc. And because I love those things, it's a place where my interests and the interests of other people overlap, and we can form friendships around them.

Remember as you reciprocate to only tweet good material. Your followers trust you to recommend something that's worth their time.

When you share or retweet, try to add something to the tweeted link.

One trick to good reciprocation is to tell people why you like what you're sharing. What's in it for them if they click?

Example #1: Jael McHenry (@jaelmchenry):

Important question, good summary. RT @elizabethscraig What Type of Edit Does Your Book Need? Bit.ly/YFrugv @MarcyKennedy

Example #2: Lisa Hall-Wilson (@LisaHallWilson):

Looking to be published by a trad publisher? A recap of all the industry changes – and why most of them are good... fb.me/Fa3OliSG

You won't always have time for this, and that's fine. Try to do it as often as possible.

WHAT SHOULDN'T WE TWEET ABOUT?

Obviously, the flip side of what we should tweet about is what we shouldn't tweet about. For the most part, you're free to tweet about whatever you want, but there are a couple of general best practices you should follow.

Just so we're clear, though, this isn't about hiding who you are. We should be open and authentic about ourselves and our beliefs. But there's a right and wrong way to do that.

For example, if you're pro-life, the *wrong* way to express that would be to rant about how every woman who has an abortion is a murderer. The *right* way to express that would be to share how excited you are to be participating in a fundraiser for an organization that helps out women who would otherwise be financially unable to raise their babies.

Do you see the difference? One seeks to hurt and tear down. The other seeks to show love and help.

So here are the areas we need to guard against.

Don't be the "all writing, all the time" channel.

Unless your audience is writers, you need to be careful how often you tweet writing-related links. Don't use my Twitter feed as an example on this one since, as a writing instructor and editor, part of my audience is writers. Kristen Lamb points out the same thing. She writes books for writers, so she's trying to reach writers as well as readers.

It's not wrong to tweet writing-related links. If you know you have other writers following you, it's a way to build camaraderie by sharing links that might also be helpful to them. Just practice balance since readers who aren't writers won't care about writing-related links. And writers who have streams filled with writing links might be craving something else.

Don't be a Debbie Downer.

If you lose a pet, your car gets a flat tire, or you're just really fed up with telemarketers, it's 100% okay to tweet about that. We're all human. We all have those days and go through rough periods.

But you don't want your Twitter account (or any part of your social media platform) to turn into a woe-is-me fest where all you talk about is how bad your life is. Sharing your struggles once in a while makes you human and relatable. Sharing them all the time makes you depressing.

Even if you're going through a rough time in your life, there's probably something positive or happy you can focus on and share.

Also, be careful of making a lot of your posts sound like you're fishing for compliments. I see this happen more on Facebook than it does on Twitter, but Twitter isn't immune to it, either. It's bad form to fish for compliments in face-to-face life, and it's equally bad form to do it on social media.

Don't constantly rant about a single topic.

We all have topics we're passionate about. If you meet me in real life, you'll quickly realize I love animals. I'm a supporter of my local humane society, and all my cats are ones I adopted as strays. I have strong opinions about what should be done to people who abuse, abandon, neglect, or otherwise fail to responsibly care for their animals.

What I don't do is constantly fill my social media accounts with those opinions. Nor do I constantly talk about those things in real life. You don't change people's minds about something by constantly badgering them with your opinions. All that constant ranting will do is make people not want to spend time with you—in real life or on social media.

Don't attack someone else or a group of people.

I'm a strong believer in "praise publicly, criticize privately." Criticizing someone in public tends to make you look bad (rather than the person you're criticizing), but beyond that, it can be hurtful, and it doesn't give the person a chance to correct a flaw or problem they might genuinely have been unaware of. You're much better to send someone a private message. And when you do, remember to be kind as well as honest.

Some people, unfortunately, go so far as to publicly attack others—calling them names or otherwise saying hurtful things (e.g., "If thus-and-so is going to continue as a reporter, she should really lose some weight. She's setting a bad example for children everywhere.") I'm sure most of you would never consider doing this, but I want this book to be thorough. This is unacceptable behavior on Twitter and is likely to get you blackballed or reprimanded by other Twitter users.

Many of us wouldn't consider criticizing or attacking an individual, but might not realize that it's equally harmful to attack a whole group of people. There's no need to say that all people of one political affiliation, faith belief, sexual orientation, or fill-in-the-blank-with-another-group are idiots, haters, racists, killers, thieves, bigots, perverts, evil, hypocrites, etc.

First of all, no group of people is homogenous. Second, you've just lost any potential readers who belong to that group of people. They're not going to want to follow you and hear themselves publicly maligned.

Third, is that what your brand is about? Everything you do on social media reflects on your career as a writer, your books, and the brand you're building. If that's the kind of brand you want, be my guest and fill your Twitter account with those kinds of tweets. Just don't ask me to follow you.

CHAPTER FOURTEEN

Writing Tweets That Get Clicked and Shared

As you continue as writers in the new era, you'll hear a lot of people talking about how social media is a waste of time or how they joined Twitter (or Facebook) and it didn't make any difference to the traffic their blog got. They didn't see an increase in the numbers of books they sold.

Here's the harsh truth. Most of those people are doing it wrong and not building relationships.

If you're not getting much traffic from Twitter, and you *have* been working on relationships, the problem might be your tweets themselves.

There is a right way and a wrong way to write tweets if you actually want other people to click them and share them. (Please note that in this chapter I'm talking about tweets that include a link. Your purpose in any tweet where you include a link is to get people to click and share.)

Before we start, though, I want to mention that I know this can seem like a lot to learn just to use Twitter effectively, but it really is like learning to ride a bike. The first time we ride a bike as kids, we're thinking about balance and peddling and keeping the handlebars straight and how hard we need to push the breaks so that we stop the bike without falling over.

Soon we don't have to think about any of that. We hop on and it comes naturally. Twitter is the same way. You'll have to think about these concepts at first, but soon, if you practice, you'll be able to do everything in this book without having to spend a lot of energy thinking about it.

So—on to writing great tweets.

KEEP YOUR TWEETS SHORT ENOUGH TO BE RETWEETED WITHOUT EDITING

We live in a rushed society, so the easier you can make it for people to retweet for you without extra work, the better.

When you write your tweet, try to keep in mind how many characters people will need to add **_RT @username:_** in front. Don't use up all 140 characters available to you.

Due to the length of my username, I know that I need to come in at least 18 characters below the 140 character limit if I want to help people easily retweet my content. In other words, I ideally aim for 120-character-or-less tweets. By coming in under 120 characters, I leave them room to add a little commentary as well.

This helps people share because they don't have to figure out how to shorten your tweet before passing it along.

You won't always be able to do this, but try to as often as you can.

WRITE FOR THE VOID THAT IS TWITTER

Twitter is unique in that your tweets don't have any context other than your hashtags. None. Your tweet is all you have to interest people enough to convince them to share it and click through.

This isn't Facebook where you can write intro sentences and which pulls in the first paragraph (or a custom written description) to display below your post.

Here's what you see on Facebook.

Room for lengthy commentary about the content of the blog

You also see either the start of the post or a custom description written by the author.

Facebook pulls in a picture to help illustrate the topic

For the same post on Twitter, you'd have...

Putting Lipstick on the Troll – The Introverted Writer via @usernameofwriter #amwriting #writetip bit.ly.linkhere

If I saw that on Twitter, I would have thought it was a post saying something negative about being an introvert. I wouldn't know enough about the content to want to click. (This is actually a post from a blog I'm subscribed to and love, and I liked the post, but when I tweeted it, I didn't use the title they gave it.)

Creativity and word plays in tweets with links don't work. If people need to read the blog post to understand your tweet, it's a bad tweet. It's a bad tweet because if people don't understand your tweet, they'll never reach the blog post you're sharing. See the catch-22?

Your tweet needs to be clear about what people will get if they click.

Writers also sometimes think that, if they give too much away in their tweet, people won't bother to read the post. The opposite is actually true. How often have you agreed to read a book without knowing the genre or at least something about the plot? Probably never.

So here's what you need to do.

MAKE A SPECIFIC PROMISE ABOUT WHAT'S IN IT FOR THE READER

You're asking someone to invest into your post the most precious commodity they have—time. We can earn more money, but once time is gone, we can't get it back.

There are three keys to making this work.

Key #1 – Be Specific

Imagine you saw this tweet:

Rocky Mountain High

Any idea what this post is going to be about? I didn't when I saw this tweet on Twitter. I clicked through just so that I could tell you. Turns out it was about the legalization of marijuana in Colorado. If I hadn't wanted to find out for this book, I wouldn't have clicked at all because I would have thought it was a post about living in the Rocky Mountains.

Here's another real tweet:

Why Not Zombies?

This is a little better, but I'm a fantasy/sci-fi fan, and this didn't compel even me to click because it was too vague. All I knew was that it would have something to do with zombies. I would have needed to know why not zombies *what*? Why not write about zombies? Why not date a zombie? Why couldn't zombies exist?

This one turned out to be a defense of writers who write zombie fiction. With a clearer title and tweet, that could have been a hot topic drawing a lot of traffic.

If your tweet is too vague, you can use all the formulas you want and it will still fall flat.

Too vague = The Shocking Truth About Doctors

About whether doctors practice what they preach? About whether doctors are stealing from their patients while under anesthetic? We don't care because we don't know what shocking truth you might be revealing.

Specific = The Shocking Truth About What Your Doctor Might Be Doing to Harm Your Health

Key #2 – Make a Promise You Can Keep

Your tweet needs to actually tell what the post is about. If you use smoke and mirrors, or it turns out that you only told a half-truth in your tweet, you lose trust.

Example: The Amazing Strategy No One Is Using to Earn Freelance Writing Gigs

I recently received a similar title in my email inbox, and I snorted in disbelief.

Really? No one is using this strategy? I instantly doubted the writer based on the title alone. I felt like I was being manipulated because surely someone was using this strategy (and successfully), at least the writer of the post, because if no one is using it, why should I bother using it? What proof does the writer have that it even works if no one is using it?

You also need to be able to deliver on your promise. Don't trick people into coming to your post with a false promise. They'll never come back.

If you make a big claim or a big promise, you need to be capable of delivering on that promise in your post.

Here's another one I pulled from my Twitter stream.

How to Go Viral Without Really Trying

When I clicked through on this post, it had nothing to do with how to go viral. It was a repeat of a post on parenting. The post was hilarious (and terrifying to anyone who doesn't yet have children), but if I wasn't already familiar with this author and his blog, I would be leery about clicking on his tweets again because it was a misrepresentation of the content. Like most people, I don't like to feel tricked, especially when my social media time is limited.

Key #3 – Give the Reader the Obvious Benefit They'll Receive from Reading the Post

What's the takeaway from your post?

Your tweet should offer to meet a need your ideal reader feels (even if they don't realize they feel it).

This could be a need for entertainment. It could be a need for a solution to a problem they have. It could be encouragement, either spiritual or psychological. It could be a combination.

The more explicit you can make the benefit, the better.

Let's say you'd written a post giving writers practical tips on how to say *no* when they were asked to do something that they didn't really have the time to do and would have to sacrifice their writing time to take part in.

Example:
Okay Tweet
Every Successful Writer Must Learn to Say "No"

You're hinting in this tweet that the benefit in your post is success. Learning to say "no" to some things will make you a more successful writer. That's okay, but why should I click through to read the whole post? What will I get in the post that the tweet hasn't already given me?

Better Tweet
Why You Need to Learn to Say "No" to Succeed as a Writer

This tweet makes the content of the post more clear. It's going to give you reasons to say *no* to some things in order to succeed at others. Better, but if I already know I need to say *no*, there's no motivation for me to click through. Where's the practical takeaway for me?

Best Tweet
Six Ways to Say "No" With Less Guilt

Everyone can tell us that we need to say *no* to be successful, but not everyone can tell us how to do it in a way that's easier and less stressful for us. That's an amazing benefit. If you wanted to be sure that people understood that the post was tips for writers, you could write "Six Ways for Writers to Say 'No' With Less Guilt."

Sometimes I see writers burying the benefit inside their post. They'll write a more "creative" tweet in the hope that it'll draw people in, and then partway into the post lay out the practical benefit. Don't do that. Give your benefit right up front. You're competing with a lot of other attention-sucking items in the world.

Here's a good example of a real tweet.

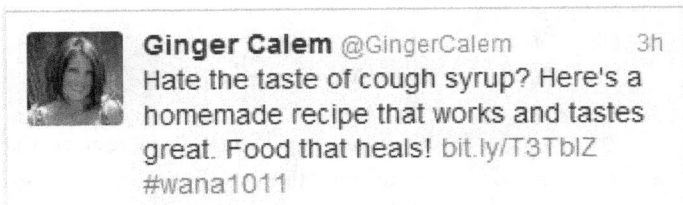

Ginger Calem @GingerCalem · 3h
Hate the taste of cough syrup? Here's a homemade recipe that works and tastes great. Food that heals! bit.ly/T3TblZ #wana1011

Ginger wrote this post and sent out this tweet in the fall. She knows this is cold season. And she knows that people will be trying to gag down nasty cough syrup. The benefit she's offering people who click through is a cough syrup recipe that not only works but tastes better as well.

Ginger also used another great technique to grab a reader's attention and get them to click through or share.

POSE A QUESTION

We all feel compelled to answer a question or to want to know the answer. It immediately gets us thinking. It's also a great trick for fiction writers who might be writing about a topic in a post that doesn't easily lend itself to an obvious takeaway.

Louise Behiel is a writer and therapist who does a lot of really deep posts on relationships, families, and childhood abuse because these are themes that feature in her fiction work.

Here are two examples of question tweets she's used.

How Deep Are the Scars of Abuse?
How Do You Define Success?

For the first one, Louise implies that the benefit you'll receive from reading her post is that you'll learn about how deeply abuse damages people.

As I've mentioned, I'm a fantasy writer, and part of my brand is showing that fantasy isn't about escaping this world. I write fantasy that helps us see life in this world in a new way and gives us a safe place to explore problems that might otherwise be too difficult to face. So part of my signature is posts where I take a life lesson from fantasy or science fiction. That's difficult to translate into a tweet, so I pose a question about the topic we'll be discussing.

Do You Ever Feel Like You Don't Fit In? (This one was about the movie *How to Train Your Dragon*.)

How Do We Know If Someone Has Truly Changed? (This one was about a character in the TV show *Once Upon A Time*.)

Do You Believe In Second Chances? (This one was about Gollum in *Lord of the Rings*.)

AROUSE THEIR CURIOSITY

Arousing curiosity is also a great trick for fiction writers if you're doing a post that's either about entertainment, education, or just something that doesn't lend itself to the previous ways to grab a reader's attention.

A fiction writer I know did a really fun post on bacon, and she titled it…"Bacon!"

When people tweeted it from her website, when she tweeted it herself, she used her title exactly. The tweets that went out said "Bacon!"

This post didn't get nearly the traffic I thought it deserved. It was entertaining, and afterwards, I wanted to go out and buy some of the quirky products she featured. A better title (and subsequent tweets) would have attracted more traffic.

Improved Tweet: More Than a Breakfast Food: Nine Unconventional Uses for Bacon

I often write about mythical creatures and draw a life lesson from them. I've used titles and tweets such as...

My Life As A Three-Headed Chimera
Are You Struggling to Control Your Inner Centaur?

These worked for me because they combined a keyword (in each post, it's the mythical creature I'm featuring), aroused curiosity, and sometimes also asked a question.

Almost anything you're writing about on your blog can fit into one of these categories for great tweets. If you find that they can't, then you need to ask if this post is reader-centric (in other words, are you writing to give to your readers?) or is it egocentric (your blog is more an online journal where you expect readers to be interested in the minutia of your life). If you want more traffic, if you're writing to build a platform, you need to be reader-centric.

On that topic, even though it's a little outside the scope of this book, I want to emphasize how important it is to try to make your blog about more than just you. This is a tricky line to walk.

You want your readers to connect to you on a personal level and get to know you, but for the most part, no one outside of your immediate family is going to care whether you're building a deck, went on vacation to the Bahamas, or met your latest word count or #ROW80 goals. That's not why people read blogs. That's why we get together with friends for coffee.

What you want to try to do is find the overlap. Where do your personal stories and interests overlap with what might be interesting to or helpful for your readers? Don't write about the fact that you built a deck. Write the funny story of what went wrong and give your readers tips for avoiding the same mistake in the future.

This depends a lot on what kind of readers you're trying to reach, too.

For me, I know my audience is going to be largely people who love science fiction and fantasy (and those are my interests, too), so I have the hard-core geek posts. I interview authors writing in those genres or I give recipes for food based on those books or feature an unbelievable but real place or creature.

But I also want to go deeper, and that's when I draw out a discussion topic or lesson from a science fiction or fantasy movie, TV show, book, mythology, etc. I know these draw in people who might not ordinarily read fantasy, but who will now be interested in my books because they've enjoyed how accessible I made science fiction and fantasy.

When you're writing your blog posts, what themes are in your books that you could carry over to your blog posts and engage your readers with? I have a friend who, shortly after she released her YA novel, wrote a post on first kisses because her protagonist experienced her first kiss in the book. That encouraged readers to share their first-kiss stories.

When we blog like that, it's going to be more fun for us and more fun for our readers, not to mention easier to tweet about.

SHARES FROM YOUR WEBSITE

I've already mentioned how important it is to have a button on the bottom of your posts that allows people to easily tweet your blog post, and how you should try to use a sharing service with a built-in link shortener.

Part of what you want from Twitter is for a symbiosis to form between it and your website. You want people to follow you from Twitter to your blog (or whatever you're using as your online home) and enjoy your content there so much that they subscribe and share your posts on Twitter so that more people follow their tweets back to your blog and the cycle continues.

Here's where this circle gets tricky.

Do you think most of these people are going to write their own tweets for your content?

Nope.

They're going to hit the share button on your site, and look what they'll tweet.

That's right. They'll be tweeting your post title, which means that when you write your title, all of the above applies.

If you want to increase your reach on Twitter, one of the best things you can do is create a title that's going to translate well to a tweet.

Bonus Tip: To increase your click-through rate, place links 25% of the way through your tweet rather than at the end. Why does this work? If your tweet is interesting, people want to be able to click the link immediately rather than sorting through the hashtags and attribution to find it. We live in an impatient society. Plus, if you accidentally make your tweet too long, you don't want what gets cut off to be the link.

CHAPTER FIFTEEN

Scheduling and Automation: Evil or Helpful?

One of the biggest debates about Twitter is whether or not to automate certain elements, whether to automate at all, whether to schedule tweets in advance, and on and on.

You'll hear a lot of authors and "social media expects" advising you to automate everything you can. Bad idea. Let me walk you through it.

DON'T AUTO-FOLLOW

If you've been on Twitter for any length of time, you've probably received a message like this after following someone new.

> Thanks for the follow! I automatically followed you back using twitterautofollowback.com! You can do the same thing for FREE!

It might sound like this is a great way to save time, but it causes more trouble than it saves. You'll end up following spammers and accounts whose tweets you don't want to see. The accounts you actually want to see will end up buried in the clutter. When that happens, you're not going to want to spend time on Twitter.

From a purely selfish perspective, following people who don't engage with you on Twitter hurts your Klout score. (If you don't know what Klout is yet, don't worry about it too much, but there's a helpful post about metrics called "Numbers Are Our Friends" by Kristen Lamb.)

DON'T AUTOMATE A DIRECT MESSAGE TO SEND TO PEOPLE WHO FOLLOW YOU

You'll hear a lot of "social media experts" advocating automated direct messages as a great way to promote yourself to new followers. They're not. I'll give you some examples.

Example 1: Thanks for following. If you'd like to know more about my books, please visit my website: bit.ly/linkhere.

Example 2: Great to connect! Would love it if you'd LIKE my Facebook fan page. Message me if I can do the same for you.

Both of these are obviously messages that have been set up to go out to every new follower. It begs the question...why should I take the time to visit your website or like your page if you couldn't take the time to type a hello to me yourself? (Not to mention that Facebook likes that are made in exchange for liking their page are absolutely worthless because the person doesn't have any real interest in you or your work. In her Facebook classes at W.A.N.A. International, Lisa Hall-Wilson talks a lot about empty likes and how they hurt your EdgeRank—the way Facebook decides what to show people.)

> Example 3: Hi Marcy, good luck with your writing. Thanks for the follow. I hope you'll enjoy my book blog at link-here.com.

This is based off a real message I received (changed slightly to protect the guilty/innocent). This one wasn't technically automated, but it's not much better. They know I'm a writer, but this is still about them. They still want something from me. This isn't how social media works. You need to give and interact before you can expect to get anything from people.

DON'T USE TRUETWIT VALIDATION (OR ANY OTHER VALIDATION SERVICE)

Validation services are external, automated services that you set up to supposedly sort out whether the people who want to follow you are real people or bots. They make people click an extra link to prove they're a real person. Again, on the surface, this seems to make sense because it could save you time and protect you from bots.

But here's the problem. You're going to cost yourself real followers. You've added an extra step that a lot of people won't take because it requires them to click an additional link that comes in a direct message. Any link like this, created by an external service, that takes you to an external site makes your account vulnerable to hacking. You're not being a good tweep by putting your new followers' accounts at risk.

Plus, let's be honest. You're not required to follow people just because they follow you, so you don't lose anything by allowing people to follow you without validating them first. And if they turn out to be pests, they're easy to block later.

SCHEDULING TWEETS

When you create a tweet, Twitter gives you the option of scheduling it. Since we've covered all the other major forms of automation, that really only leaves us one question—should we schedule tweets or not?

I'm not against the occasional scheduled tweet, but I think we need to be careful about it.

We should never add hashtags to scheduled tweets because we risk clogging up a slow-moving column, but scheduling a few tweets can help us manage our time better.

For example, if I have a lot of great links I want to share, I might not want to tweet them all in the 5–10 minutes I have today to spend on Twitter. If I send them all out in that timeframe, I'm going to take over the columns of people who might not be following that many people. Do I just not share the links, then? Or wait until tomorrow and hope I haven't forgotten them? In this case, I think it's better to spread them out by scheduling them. This also allows me to use more of the time I'm on Twitter for conversations.

But there's the crux of the matter. Scheduling tweets shouldn't be used in place of actually being on Twitter. You need to be there, interacting. If you're not there, you're once again asking people to do something you're not willing to do. What if everyone scheduled tweets but never spent time on Twitter? Who would see all those scheduled tweets? Twitter would be worthless.

In the end, a little authentic time on Twitter is better than a constant stream of automated messages.

Time Management on Twitter

Before I move on to some advanced Twitter strategies, I'm going to cover time management on Twitter. That way, if you're new to Twitter and want to stop reading until you're more comfortable, you'll have everything you need and can return to the advanced chapters when you're ready.

You don't need to spend all day on social media or give up large chunks of your writing time to build a strong platform. That's a fallacy. Between Facebook, Twitter, and Google+, I usually spend less than 30 minutes a day. (This is my average. Some days I'm not on social media at all. Other days, I'll spend more time.)

So how can you make this all work in such a small amount of time?

FOUR TIPS TO START

Set a Time Limit

This is safer than saying you only want to make a certain number of tweets a day. Limiting tweets limits your potential for conversation, and without conversation, you'll find it very difficult to make quality connections.

Do Social Media at Your Worst Time of Day

I try to stay off social media during the afternoon and early evening because that's when I write best. Know your own best time and shut off all social media at that point. Instead, spend time on Twitter when you're not at your best. You'll most frequently see me on in the morning or late at night.

The idea is that, because Twitter should be fun, it allows you to still do something to forward your career even during your least productive times. Having some time to chat can also help you perk up if you're feeling discouraged or tired.

Take a Day Off

You don't need to panic if you can't be on Twitter every day. If you were to scroll back through my tweets, you'd notice that some days I'm not on at all. Some days I'm only on long enough to thank people for RTing for me.

It doesn't hurt you to take a day off (or a week off) if you're simply too busy to have meaningful interactions. In fact, I encourage you to set aside one day a week where you don't do any social media. It's too easy for us to get stressed out and allow the tools we should be using to control us. A dedicated social media-free day gives you a day without the stress of feeling like you need to be building your platform every spare minute.

Use Twitter as a Reward

One of the things that I've found works for me and ensures that I'm not neglecting my writing in favor of social media is to use Twitter as a reward. I set a goal, and when I reach that goal, I go online for 5–10 minutes and chat. Doing it this way helps me stay focused on my work during work time. We're actually more productive if we take a 5–10 minute break every hour than if we try to work without stopping for hours on end.

HOW TO USE TWITTER WITH LIMITED TIME

I'm going to give you a few patterns you can use if you only have 5–10 minutes a day for Twitter. You don't have to follow these patterns exactly. I'm providing them to you to help you get started. If they don't work for you, take the parts that do, and don't worry about the parts that don't.

My personal opinion (backed up by my experience) is that you'll get the most out of Twitter if you're able to spend 15 minutes or more a day. If you think that's impossible, start to brainstorm times that are otherwise wasted and use those for Twitter. I can often set up my laptop in the kitchen while I'm cooking dinner. I need to keep an eye on the food anyway, so I can't go far. It's the perfect time to get some social media time in.

If you spend a lot of time waiting for appointments or watching your kids play sports, you can download Hootsuite onto your phone and sneak in some social media time.

Get creative, and you'll find that Twitter doesn't take away from anything else.

However, if you absolutely only have 5–10 minutes and can't squeeze it in during otherwise wasted minutes, here are the patterns I promised.

Twitter in 5 Minutes a Day

If you only have 5 or even 10 minutes a day for Twitter, you might find it easier to sit down once a week and plan out your promotion and reciprocation tweets in advance. This is a time management trick known as *batching*, where you do similar tasks at the same time. Rather than scrambling to find something to tweet and wasting a lot of time looking for material, you'll be able to focus your online time on conversation.

If you only have 5 minutes a day to spend on Twitter, you're going to have to allocate your time a little differently than if you had more time. Below, I've given you a sample pattern to use. If you use the A, B, and C patterns twice each week, you'll be able to cover all your bases on Twitter.

Day A

(1 minute) Share a link to one of your blog posts or to one of your books.

(1 minute) Share a link to someone else's content. This could be a blog post you read and loved or a retweet of a tweet with a link that you see while on Twitter.

(1 minute) Reply to any @ messages sent to you that need a reply.

(2 minutes) Start or join in a conversation on #MyWANA or another writing hashtag.

Day B

(1 minute) Share a link to one of your blog posts or to one of your books.

(1 minute) Reply to any @ messages sent to you that need a reply.

(3 minutes) Focus on one of your lists. Use this list to retweet for two to three people and to join in a conversation or reply to something someone has tweeted.

Day C

(1 minute) Share a link to one of your blog posts or to one of your books.

(1 minute) Reply to any @ messages sent to you that need a reply.

(3 minutes) Focus on one of your non-writing columns. You may not find material you can RT in this column. Try instead to join a conversation or to reply to a couple new people.

I know I called this Twitter in 5 minutes a day, but as people start to follow you or as you find people you want to follow, you'll want to set aside one additional minute to take care of this. In the grand scheme of things, one extra minute shouldn't be a problem.

Twitter in 10 Minutes a Day

(1 minute) Share a link to one of your blog posts or to one of your books.

(1 minute) Reply to any @ messages sent to you that need a reply.

(1 minute) Follow one new person, and check out and follow anyone who has followed you.

(3 minutes) Tweet something that could start a conversation, and engage with the people who reply.

(1 minute) Share a link to an article/blog post that would interest future potential readers. Remember to add hashtags.

(3 minutes) Choose one of the options below.

Option A

Focus on one of your columns. You may not find material you can RT in this column. Try instead to join a conversation or to reply to a couple new people. Each day, choose a new column. If you have three good columns, this allows you to visit each of them once a week.

Option B

Focus on one of your lists. Use this list to retweet for two to three people and to join a conversation or reply to something someone has tweeted. If you have three good lists, this allows you to visit each of them once a week.

Once you've been actively using Twitter for a while, you'll find the patterns that work best for you.

If you only have a limited amount of time each day, and can only be on Twitter once a day, try to also vary the time. For example, on Monday, log on in the morning; on Tuesday, log on in the afternoon; and on Wednesday, log on in the evening. This allows you to meet and interact with more people.

PART THREE

Advanced Techniques

Using Click to Tweet

I f you're brand new to Twitter, we've now covered everything you need to know to build a solid author platform on Twitter. The rest of the book is going to be advanced techniques that you don't really need but can help you get even more out of Twitter and add a new dimension to how you're using it in your overall platform-building strategy.

The first of those strategies is Click to Tweet.

Without even realizing it, you've probably seen Click to Tweet used by big bloggers.

It allows you to write a custom tweet that people can then share on Twitter, and it can exponentially increase the number of times your blog posts are shared. People on Twitter love to tweet and re-tweet quotable material.

Let me give you an example.

I wrote a post on the movie *MegaMind*, titled "Is Praise More Powerful than Criticism?" After I wrote the post, I found a line that I thought would resonate with people and that they might want to share.

We can't change anyone, but we can be the catalyst for them wanting to change. (Click here to tweet this.)

If you were to click where it says *Click here to tweet this*, your twitter account would open and you'd have the option to tweet the prepared tweet I created that looks like this...

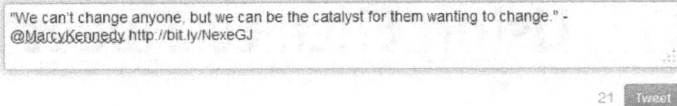

> "We can't change anyone, but we can be the catalyst for them wanting to change." -
> @MarcyKennedy http://bit.ly/NexeGJ
>
> 21 Tweet

Here's another example from a post I did on showing vs. telling in fiction.

Tight writing has less to do with the number of words used and more to do with making every word count. (Click here if you'd like to tweet that.)

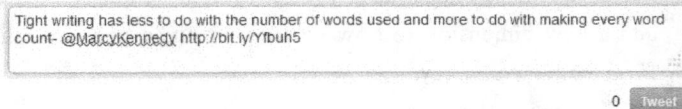

> Tight writing has less to do with the number of words used and more to do with making every word
> count- @MarcyKennedy http://bit.ly/Yfbuh5
>
> 0 Tweet

You can see that I usually use the **anchor text** (the stuff in parentheses) of *Click here if you'd like to tweet that.*

What you use is up to you.

Some other options for anchor text include...

Click to tweet
Tweet that
Want to tweet that?

Obviously, there are tricks to making this work, so I'll walk you through the process from start to finish.

Step 1: Think about short, tweetable sentences while you write your blog posts. This only works if you can come up with something pithy that will fit within the tweet with room left for at least a short link. I like to leave room for a short link and my username.

Step 2: Finish your blog post and schedule it. This step is very important. Do **not** skip it. You can still update your post once it's scheduled. The reason you need to schedule your post first is to set your permalink. You'll need this permalink to create your custom tweet.

Step 3: Copy your permalink. If you're on a Wordpress site, the back side where you write your posts should look like this.

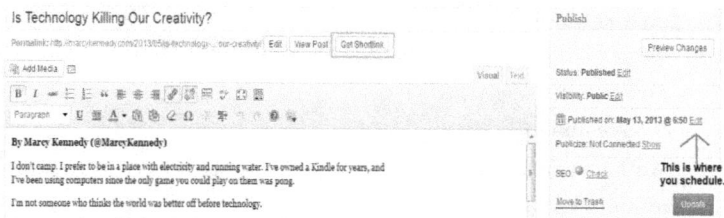

I've added an arrow pointing to where you'd schedule your blog for a certain day and time if you've never done this before. Once you've selected a date and time, the blue **Publish** button—directly below my arrow—will turn to a **Schedule** button. When you schedule, it turns into an **Update** button, which is what you see in my screen shot.

If you don't want to use the short link generated by your JetPack plug-in or if you aren't using JetPack and so you only have the long link, you can take your long link to Bitly.com and manually shorten it.

However you do it, make sure you have a shortened link copied.

Step 4: Go to www.clicktotweet.com. You'll see a box that looks a little like the **Compose** box on TweetDeck or Hootsuite.

Step 5: Paste your shortened link into the box.

Step 6: Go back to your post and copy the quote you want to include. Paste it into the box in front of your shortened link.

Step 7: If you have enough characters left, add your @username. You'll know how many characters you have thanks to the number to the bottom left of the box.

Step 8: Click *Generate Link!*

Step 9: Copy the link it generates and take it back to your post.

Step 10: Write your anchor text, and add in the link Click to Tweet generated the same way that you'd add a link if you wanted to link to another website. When you do this, I recommend choosing to open the link in a new tab because, even though you want people to share, you don't want them to leave your website.

Step 11: Click *Update* to save.

You're done!

And now that you know how to use Click to Tweet, you can use it any time you want to custom make a tweet for people to share—for example, during the launch of your next book.

CHAPTER EIGHTEEN

Figuring Out When Your Followers Are Online

I n previous chapters, we talked about the evils of scheduling and automation, and about how to make the most of your time if you can only be on Twitter for 5–10 minutes a day.

If you can only be on Twitter for a very limited amount of time, as often as possible, you'll want to have that time be when the majority of your followers are actively online.

That's not something you can easily tell just by looking at your Twitter stream. A helpful tool that will generate a report for you is http://www.tweriod.com/.

Tweriod analyzes your and your followers' tweets and generates a report. The length of time it takes to generate a report varies based on how many followers you have. They say it normally takes an hour or two, but I received mine in less than 20 minutes (and I have a fair few followers).

They'll send you an email letting you know your report is ready.

Once you get the email, click the link to take you back to Tweriod. It'll ask you to sign in with your Twitter account, but their user interface isn't as clear as it could be. To sign in once your report has been generated, click the blue button that's half obscured in the middle of the page. I think it's meant to say **Go to Dashboard**.

Once you're into your dashboard, click on the green button that says **My Analysis**.

The report breaks down into Sundays, Mondays, Weekends, and Weekdays. It'll tell you the time range when your tweets get the most exposure and also show you a graph of when most of your users are online.

For example, here's my weekday graph.

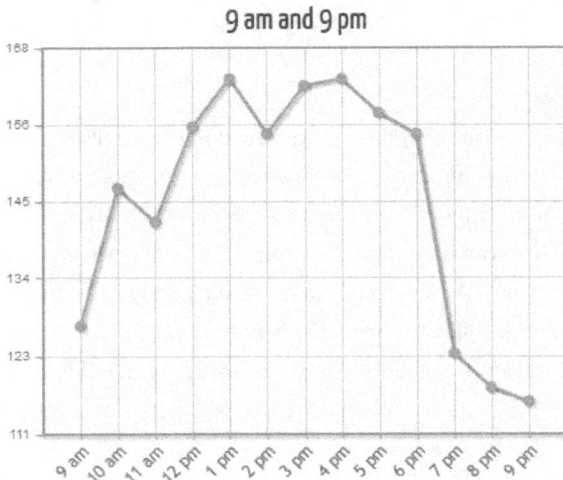

It tracks between 9 am and 9 pm Eastern (the time zone is determined by whatever time zone you've set on your Twitter profile). I can see that the majority of my followers are on Twitter at 1 pm and again between 3 pm and 4 pm. So now I know that if I want to reach and talk to the largest number of my Twitter followers, those are the best times for me to try to stop in.

As you look through the results, the two things you really want to be thinking about are "When is it best for me to be online?" and "When is it the worst time for me to be online?"

Tweriod has a premium analysis, but I've never used it. The free analysis is plenty for your needs as writers. The only real drawback to the free service is that they limit you to generating one report a month. And really, you're not likely to need a report more than once a month.

IS THERE A BEST TIME OVERALL TO BE ON TWITTER?

Yes and no.

Statistically speaking, tweets made between 2 pm and 6 pm Eastern receive a higher click-through rate than tweets made in the morning because this is when all the time zones across the U.S. and Canada overlap with daytime hours after 9 am. Unlike Facebook, Twitter has a very high daytime population.

This isn't to say that people aren't on Twitter in the evenings or on weekends. They are, but there are fewer of them.

Fewer people online can actually work in your favor. Your tweets are more likely to be seen in columns when there are fewer people tweeting.

In other words, it's fun to take a look at when the majority of people are online, but I wouldn't worry about it. Talk to whoever is online when you're online. You'll meet great people in Australia, the United Kingdom, Poland, the Netherlands, and all across the world.

CHAPTER NINETEEN

Using Images on Twitter

When it comes to using images on any social media site (including our blogs), there are two things we need to consider before we talk about how and when to use them—safety and legality.

We've already talked in an earlier chapter about safety when using photos we've taken ourselves. If we're not using images we've taken, then we'll need to find images to use.

The biggest concern among writers is about where to find photos to use that are both free and legal. Most of us don't have money to spend buying images for social media use, but we also don't want to infringe on someone else's copyright.

With the help of my shutterbug friend Melinda VanLone, I've put together a list of seven free and legal places to get images. (If you don't yet know Melinda, she writes urban fantasy, and you can find her on Twitter as @MelindaVan or on her website www.melindavan.com.)

Free Images

URL: http://www.freeimages.com/

The photos here are provided free of charge. There's a link with each image detailing what you are and aren't allowed to do with it. The force behind this site is Getty images and iStockPhoto (both pay sites that are powerhouses in the stock photo industry), which means you can be sure they've done the best they can to make sure you don't end up in trouble.

Free Digital Photos

URL: http://www.freedigitalphotos.net

This site offers photos both for free and for a fee, depending on what you want to do with the image. Some will be offered free but have a watermark (a light imprint indicating the photographer), or you can pay a small fee for a watermark-free version. They also let you pin most of their images to Pinterest.

Morgue File

URL: http://www.morguefile.com/

They don't have the biggest selection, and the quality is sometimes a bit dubious, but the price is right and the license is generous (you can use them on your website/book cover/business card, you can alter the image as you wish, etc.). Most don't even require attribution.

Open Photo

URL: http://openphoto.net

The user interface on this site is clunky. To download the image, look for a tiny link below it. Each image explains what they'd like in return, such as attribution or a link.

Flickr

URL: http://www.flickr.com

Not every image is available for use, of course, but there are plenty that are, and they are free with just an attribution. They offer a helpful explanation of the Creative Commons license in easy-to-understand language at http://www.flickr.com/creativecommons/. Kristen Lamb has also opened a *WANACommons* group on Flickr. Contribute the photos you're willing to share, and feel free to use without fear any photos from this group.

Wikimedia Commons

URL: http://commons.wikimedia.org/wiki/Main_Page

This is a database of free media files (under a Creative Commons license) to which anyone can contribute. Each image (or piece of media) will list the license restrictions. Be careful to read each license carefully, since not every photo is free to use in all circumstances.

Every Stock Photo

URL: http://www.everystockphoto.com/

This is a license-specific photo search engine. They index and search millions of freely licensed photos, from many sources, and present them in an integrated search. The license is listed with each image, and each is different, so be sure to read what you're allowed to do. They do not host the images themselves. They simply help you search.

IMAGES ON TWEETDECK VS. HOOTSUITE

Before we talk about how to upload images on TweetDeck or Hootsuite, I do want to talk about one difference so that people using Hootsuite don't think they're doing it wrong.

Hootsuite doesn't automatically display images.

Here's a picture tweet I did to show you the difference.

From Hootsuite...

MarcyKennedy
1:41pm via TweetDeck
The monster zucchini continues! We're now
busy making zucchini and curry soup :)
pic.twitter.com/jct8Hkfdbk

From TweetDeck...

Marcy Kennedy @MarcyKen... 8m
The monster zucchini continues!
We're now busy making zucchini
and curry soup :)
pic.twitter.com/jct8Hkfdbk

Details

You can see how images stand out more on TweetDeck and give a more pleasant experience.

I'm hoping Hootsuite changes this because I love the added visual pop from seeing pictures in my stream.

This is information for you to know, but not something you need to worry about (unless you want to email Hootsuite and tell them you want this to change). You have no control over what app people use to access Twitter.

However, this is why I highly recommend that you add a tweet to go with the images you upload. People aren't likely to click the pic link in Hootsuite without something to tempt them to do so.

So now it's time to talk about the nuts-and-bolts how-to.

HOW TO ATTACH A PHOTO USING TWEETDECK

Attaching a photo wasn't always possible. It certainly wasn't as easy as it is now. But in their attempt to stay competitive with Instagram, Twitter (and the related apps) have made it simple to do.

Step 1: Click **New Tweet**. (This may also be called **Compose**. TweetDeck switches between the two when they make updates.)

Step 2: When the box opens, look right before the spot where you'd write your tweet. You'll see a little icon that looks like a camera and the words **Add Image**. When you click that button, a new box will open so you can select the image you want from your computer.

Your photo must be 3MB or less.

Step 3: Upload your picture. Once you upload, you'll be returned to the **Compose** box on Twitter, where you can add a tweet to go along with the photo. The 140-character limit still applies.

HOW TO ATTACH A PHOTO USING HOOTSUITE

Step 1: Click in the **Compose Tweet** box.

Step 2: Click the paperclip icon. That will allow you to select an image/file from your computer to attach. I've circled it below.

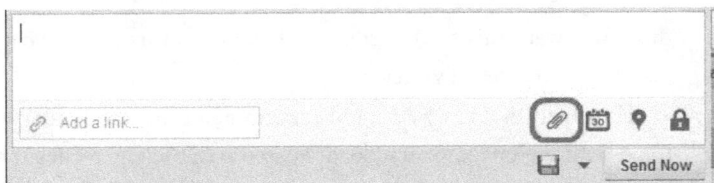

Step 3: Upload your picture. Once you upload, Hootsuite will add it as a link to your tweet. You can then write your tweet around it. The 140-character limit still applies.

WHY SHOULD WE BOTHER WITH IMAGES ON TWITTER?

The appeal of Twitter is the quick, 140-character text bites, and so some people struggle to see why we should try to occasionally add images.

As a writer building a platform, here's the bottom line—we should at least try it because so few people are doing it right now.

In other words, it's a fun, easy way to stand out from the crowd. If you can find images that your followers and ideal readers would enjoy, then it's a great way to make your Twitter stream something unique they want to follow and interact with. They can be great conversation starters.

In a mass of text, look how one image can stand out.

If you imagine this column on TweetDeck, where all the columns around it are text, you can see how your gaze is drawn to the picture of the dogs.

WHAT IMAGES SHOULD I SHARE?

The answer to this depends on what you write and where you are in your career.

An author with a large fan base might want to share bits of their writing experience, like pictures of their office, pictures from events, or even pictures of their scribbled-on draft of the next book.

For those still building a fan base, you're better to connect as people and share your passions (being wise, of course, about how much we let the whole world know about where we live and our private lives—remember what I said earlier about safety). If you're a painter, do a craft, or are an avid cook, you can share your latest project. If you garden, do a daily or weekly picture from your garden. Do you love cute kitten pictures? Someone else probably does, too.

We could also share pictures that we know will appeal specifically to our ideal reader for our books.

If you write chick lit, share some pictures of the great find from your latest shopping trip or a yummy-looking pastry from the local coffee shop.

If you write thrillers, suspense, mysteries, or horror, you could keep an eye out for creepy-looking locations and share those.

As a fantasy writer, I'm experimenting with some of the things that have done well for me on other sites, such as "Vote: Real or Not Real" and "What Do You Think This Is?"

Or perhaps you've noticed your ideal readership enjoys quotes. Find a free-to-use image, add a quote to it, and share that.

Don't be afraid to experiment and find what's fun for you and the people following you.

CHAPTER TWENTY

Keys to Successful Twitter Events

For the final chapter, we come to Twitter events. Twitter events usually come in two types—a single "party" or an ongoing chat. I'm going to talk about ongoing chats first.

TIPS FOR RUNNING A REGULAR TWITTER CHAT

If you remember our hashtag chapter, two of the genre-specific hashtags I gave you were for authors writing in those genres to connect at a regularly scheduled weekly chat. Well, now we're going to talk about how to start your own.

You need to be aware going in that a regular Twitter chat is a long-term commitment. This is why I discuss this as an advanced strategy. Before you think about launching a regular chat, you need to be comfortable on Twitter, and it helps if you've already built up a following of 400+ people.

It's a long-term commitment because it takes time to grow, have word of mouth spread, and build up a loyal attendance.

In other words, a regular Twitter chat isn't something you try to launch a week before your book comes out because you think it will help sell copies.

A regular Twitter chat is something you should only consider if you're genuinely passionate about a topic that many people will want to discuss.

A regular Twitter chat is usually a better fit for non-fiction authors than for fiction authors. The reason is simple. A non-fiction book is already going to hopefully be geared toward solving a problem that people perceive they have. You could host a weekly chat with tips for working moms, a healthy recipe swap (with a given ingredient being the core of each week), a discussion of a different biblical passage, financial planning tips, etc. Whatever the topic of your non-fiction book, you should be able to center a Twitter chat around it. As a non-fiction author, hosting a regular Twitter chat can help establish you as an expert in your field, as well as grow your platform.

For fiction authors, regular Twitter chats aren't going to be as directly beneficial. We're not going to build a regular Twitter chat around our fantasy world/science fiction planet or around our mystery sleuth. If fans decide to do that on their own, that's fine, but it becomes extremely egocentric and "Me! Me! Me!" if we try to organize something like that ourselves.

Because there's not going to be a direct connect between our book(s) and our Twitter chat topic, we need to think carefully about return on time investment. If we're organizing a Twitter chat because we think it will sell our novels, we should walk away and do something else. If we're organizing a Twitter chat because it'll help us meet people who share our passions and build relationships, then it can be a good way to spend our time on Twitter.

So, for example, if you're a historical fiction author who writes novels set in a particular time period and you love researching that era, you might want to start a chat where people get together to discuss particular questions about that era. You could bring in university professors who teach about that time period or discuss other books and movies set then.

Another example that could work for a fiction author is to start a chat where each week they talk about a different book from their genre (not their own book). It becomes much like a Twitter-based book club.

Neither of these is going to be directly about your book. This is not a sales tactic where you pitch your book to readers. It's about people with similar interests getting together to enjoy their shared passion. I can't stress this enough because, if you turn your chat into a pitch for your book, you'll immediately lose people.

So now that I've given you the overview and disclaimer, here's what you need to do if you want to launch a regular Twitter chat.

Research and Select a Hashtag

Regular Twitter chats are always based around a hashtag. People turn that hashtag into a column/stream, and that's how they keep an eye on the chat. When choosing a hashtag, you need to try to select one that's not being used yet (ideal) or isn't being actively used (second-best option). You'll also want to take length into consideration. The shorter the hashtag, the better, because it leaves more room for attendees to write their tweets.

Set a Day and Time

Regular Twitter chats are...regular. They're always Fridays from 3:00–4:00 pm Eastern or Tuesdays from 7:00–8:00 pm Pacific. People come to count on them, and if you aren't consistent, your Twitter chat will fail. When you pick your day and time, keep in mind that more people are online on weekdays than on weekends. Also take into consideration the overlap between time zones. A chat set at 8:00 pm Pacific is 11:00 pm Eastern. Always specify time zone to avoid confusion.

Establish a Page on Your Website/Blog

If you're going to be doing a regular Twitter chat, it's important to have a permanent page on your website/blog that you can point people to that gives them the hashtag and the date and time, and tells them what the chat will be about. If you plan topics in advance, this is also where you can list upcoming topics for the chats (a highly recommended practice).

Post a Schedule

I do recommend posting a schedule of your planned topics because it helps build excitement in attendees. They come ready to talk about a particular topic. But from a planning perspective, this also guarantees that you don't get to the chat, draw a blank, and leave people feeling like you've wasted their time. Even if you choose not to post your planned topics, you should still plan at least a month in advance in order to schedule and announce any special guests (e.g., subject matter experts).

Decide Whether You're Going to Provide a Transcript Post-Chat

Many regular Twitter chats archive (either in summary or using a service like http://storify.com/) their chats so that people who missed one can get caught up, or so that people who aren't sure they want to attend can poke around before investing their time.

TIPS FOR RUNNING A TWITTER PARTY

Twitter parties to celebrate a book launch or some other special event are much more common than regular Twitter chats because they're a smaller time investment on the part of the organizer and the attendees. Most Twitter parties are three hours in length (though I've seen some that run all day, with people popping in and out as they're able). As the organizer/guest of honor, you should be present at the Twitter party the whole time it's running.

Twitter parties come with their own unique set of challenges. If very few people show up, the hashtag will look abandoned and then new people who do come will float away without engaging. It becomes a self-defeating cycle. I can't promise you a successful Twitter party any more than I can promise you a best-selling book, but I can give you some tips for having the best chance of success.

Research and Select a Hashtag

The first step is the same as for a regular Twitter chat. People turn that hashtag into a column/stream, and that's how they keep an eye on the party. When choosing a hashtag, you need to try to select one that's not being used yet (ideal) or isn't being actively used (second-best option). You'll also want to take length into consideration. The shorter the hashtag, the better, because it leaves more room for attendees to write their tweets.

Set a Day and Time

Whereas the regular length for a Twitter chat is one hour, Twitter parties normally run three hours. You can run a longer Twitter event, but I don't recommend doing so your first time. Three hours is better for first-time Twitter party organizers in part because it's easier to keep momentum going for that length of time than for a day-long event, but it's also long enough that you're able to hit the sweet spot for more time zones. Similarly to a regular Twitter chat, make sure to clearly list the date, time, and time zone—e.g., Monday, July 29, from 3:00–6:00 pm Eastern.

Begin to Build Buzz a Month in Advance

Don't swamp people with announcements about your Twitter party. Doing so would be very much like swamping people with tweets about your book (bad etiquette). What you want to do instead is put in the sidebar of your blog, where people will see it when they visit, an image announcing the party. You can also tell your blog followers and/or newsletter subscribers. You'll remind them again a week before and a day before. The day of the party, you'll want to tell your social media followers (giving them an hour's advance notice and then a five-minute shout out).

Enlist Friends to Help

A Twitter party that looks dead scares people away. The best way to be sure your Twitter party looks active enough that people want to stick around once they swing by is to ask for help from three to six friends. These friends agree to tweet about the party right before it starts and to hang around and chat. You can make it fun by giving them rolls to play as well. For example, at some of the Twitter parties I've attended, one person was designated the "DJ." She found songs on YouTube and shared the links on Twitter on the party hashtag. At another party I participated in, I was the "bartender," manning the coffee maker and handing out digital desserts. Obviously it's not the same as at a real party, but it gives it an active feel when the "bartender" greets new people and the "DJ" sends out songs that people can listen to on their computers, knowing other people are listening to the same song.

Be sure that you're prepared to do the same for these friends should they run a Twitter party, and it's also nice to give them a little thank-you, like a free ebook copy of your book.

At another Twitter event I organized (a one-time chat about what type of book endings people most enjoy—e.g., happy, hopeful, realistic/sad, or open-ended), four of us joined together to run the event. Because there were four of us to begin with, the party immediately looked populated. Running a joint event in this way can be great for taking the pressure off and making it more fun.

Give Away Prizes

Twitter parties are more active and more fun when you play games and offer prizes. These could be trivia contests, blog scavenger hunts (with the help of participating bloggers), name-that-movie-line, or photo caption contests. You're really only limited by your creativity. Try to think up games that could relate to your book in some way.

The trick with games is to have them planned and organized in advance so that you don't have to be scrambling during the Twitter party to come up with something. This leaves you free to interact with your guests and makes sure that you space the games evenly—having one every 30 minutes, for example.

I recommend having a Word document where you create and save the tweets related to the game, and also creating a folder on your computer where you can save any photos you plan to use.

You can also offer a grand prize (e.g., a $25 Amazon gift card) at the end of the party for anyone who participated in a game during the party. It's up to you whether the winner has to be present at the time of the draw to win or if they only needed to be a participant at some point during the event to qualify.

The essential items to remember when having games and prizes are to make the rules clear and to follow through promptly on delivering the prizes.

Establish a Page on Your Website/Blog

This is optional. You usually only need to set up a page on your website/blog for the party if you're going to have games. If you are going to run games, I recommend listing them on this page, giving a one- or two-sentence description of the game and the rules, and specifying the time block that it will run. You can also tell people what prize will be available to the winner. This helps because, if people know they can't be there the whole time, they're able to try to show up for a particular game or prize.

Do you remember when we were setting up your Twitter account and I recommended that you ignore the widget creator that would allow you to stream a public hashtag column on your website? The one exception to this is if you host a regular Twitter chat or are running a Twitter party. In that case, you might want to consider adding this to your website either temporarily (for the Twitter party) or permanently (for the regular Twitter chat).

The Two Most Important Things to Remember

You've reached the end of this crash course in Twitter. I hope you're now more comfortable with Twitter and can see ways to work it into your routine and have fun with it. Remember that building a social media platform really comes down to two things: relationships and sustainability. If you remember those two things, you'll be okay.

For links to all the resources recommended in this book and a printable copy of the suggestions in the chapter on time management, please go to www.marcykennedy.com/twitter and use the password below.

Password: **tweetme**

For People With the Old Twitter Design

Because Twitter is always changing their design options, some of you might still have the old layout and want to keep it. This section is for you.

CREATING YOUR CUSTOM BACKGROUND

Under your settings, go to *Design*.

Twitter provides you with some pre-made backgrounds for your page. They're okay, but they're nothing special, and you're not likely to find one that feels right for you and your brand.

The good news is that, if you scroll down, Twitter also gives you the option to customize your own.

Background images must be in PNG, GIF, or JPG format and smaller than 2 MB. You can't upload animated images.

(You might see people who have animated images on Twitter. They were grandfathered in when Twitter disallowed animation in

2012. So they get to keep theirs, but no one can upload any new animated images.)

Here are two good examples of how people have used their backgrounds to tell followers about their books/writing:

Kristen Lamb (@KristenLambTX) – Kristen has multiple books out, so instead of putting up the cover of one, she's created a neat little sidebar that lists both titles and lets us know they were bestsellers.

Janice Hardy (@Janice_Hardy) – Janice has three books out. She's used part of the cover image from her first book as the base of her background because of how well it represents the world of her books, and then she's added, along the side, thumbnail images of each of her individual books.

If you check the box for *Tile Background*, your image will repeat across your background. (You can see this on Janice's page.) Try it out. Whether you like this look or not is really up to you. I like a single image because I think it draws the eye more.

If you're going to use the cover of your book as your background, make sure the whole title is visible.

This is a common mistake, and a waste of your background. If you're going to upload your book cover and choose Tile Background, make sure people can see the whole title.

Underneath where you upload the image, you'll see a few other options.

Background position is just what it sounds like. Where do you want your image to appear if you don't choose Tile Background?

Background color is what shows up behind your image if it isn't large enough to cover the entire background, and *link color* is what you see on anything clickable. You can change the background and link colors by clicking the block of color, and then adjusting via the pop out box.

Overlay is that transparent film you see to the left of the area where you're making these choices.

If you don't have a book out yet, I recommend not bothering with uploading a custom background of your own making. It's not a good time investment. People will go to your page on Twitter.com once, if ever.

WHERE CAN YOU FIND FREE CUSTOM BACKGROUNDS?

Instead of trying to design your own background or using one of the generic ones Twitter offers, you can find free backgrounds from one of the following sites:

www.twittergallery.com/

Ignore the ad at the top and scroll down. They'll ask for your username and password. Make sure you change your password after you've installed your background.

ww.twitbacks.com/

If you're a little more tech-savvy, you could also use www.twitbacks.com/ to customize a background.

Most of these sites offer both paid and free options.

Under their pre-made themes, Twitter also now links you to Themeleon, where you can do all sorts of color and pattern customization.

I'll leave it up to you whether this is the best use of your time or not, but remember what I said above—people usually go to your Twitter page once, if ever.

Other Books by Marcy Kennedy

For Writers

Grammar for Fiction Writers

The world of grammar is huge, but fiction writers don't need to know all the nuances to write well. In fact, some of the rules you were taught in English class will actually hurt your fiction writing, not help it. *Grammar for Fiction Writers* won't teach you things you don't need to know. It's all about the grammar that's relevant to you as you write your novels and short stories.

Here's what you'll find inside:

- *Punctuation Basics* including the special uses of dashes and ellipses in fiction, common comma problems, how to format your dialogue, and untangling possessives and contractions.

- *Knowing What Your Words Mean and What They Don't* including commonly confused words, imaginary words and phrases, how to catch and strengthen weak words, and using connotation and denotation to add powerful subtext to your writing.

- *Grammar Rules Every Writer Needs to Know and Follow* such as maintaining an active voice and making the best use of all the tenses for fast-paced writing that feels immediate and draws the reader in.

- *Special Challenges for Fiction Writers* like reversing cause and effect, characters who are unintentionally doing the impossible, and orphaned dialogue and pronouns.
- *Grammar "Rules" You Can Safely Ignore When Writing Fiction*

Mastering Showing and Telling in Your Fiction

You've heard the advice "show, don't tell" until you can't stand to hear it anymore. Yet fiction writers of all levels still seem to struggle with it.

There are three reasons for this. The first is that this isn't an absolute rule. Telling isn't always wrong. The second is that we lack a clear way of understanding the difference between showing and telling. The third is that we're told "show, don't tell," but we're often left without practical ways to know how and when to do that, and how and when not to. So that's what this book is about.

Chapter One defines showing and telling, and explains why showing is normally better.

Chapter Two gives you eight practical ways to find telling that needs to be changed to showing, and guides you in understanding how to make those changes.

Chapter Three explains how telling can function as a useful first-draft tool.

Chapter Four goes in-depth on the seven situations when telling might be a better choice than showing.

Chapter Five provides you with practical editing tips to help you take what you've learned to the pages of your current novel or short story.

Mastering Showing and Telling in Your Fiction: A Busy Writer's Guide also includes three appendices covering how to use *The Emotion Thesaurus,* dissecting an example so you can see the concepts of showing vs. telling in action, and explaining the closely related topic of As-You-Know-Bob Syndrome.

How to Write Dialogue

How do you properly format dialogue? How can you write dialogue unique to each of your characters? Is it okay to start a chapter with dialogue? Writers all agree that great dialogue helps make great fiction, but it's not as easy to write as it looks.

In *How to Write Dialogue: A Busy Writer's Guide*, you'll learn

- how to format your dialogue,
- how to add variety to your dialogue so it's not always "on the nose,"
- when you should use dialogue and when you shouldn't,
- how to convey information through dialogue without falling prey to As-You-Know-Bob Syndrome,
- how to write dialogue unique to each of your characters,
- how to add tension to your dialogue,
- whether it's ever okay to start a chapter with dialogue,
- ways to handle contractions (or a lack thereof) in science fiction, fantasy, and historical fiction,
- tricks for handling dialect,
- and much more!

Each book in the *Busy Writer's Guide* series is intended to give you enough theory so that you can understand why things work and why they don't, but also enough examples to see how that theory looks in practice. In addition, they provide tips and exercises to help you take it to the pages of your own story with an editor's-eye view.

Strong Female Characters - A Mini-Book

The misconceptions around what writers mean when we talk about strong female characters make them one of the most difficult

212 | MARCY KENNEDY

character types to write well. Do we have to strip away all femininity to make a female character strong? How do we keep a strong female character likeable? If we're writing historical fiction or science fiction or fantasy based on a historical culture, how far can we stray from the historical records when creating our female characters?

In *Strong Female Characters: A Busy Writer's Guide*, you'll learn

- what "strong female characters" means,
- the keys to writing characters who don't match stereotypical male or female qualities,
- how to keep strong female characters likeable, and
- what roles women actually played in history.

How to Write Faster - A Mini-Book

In *How to Write Faster: A Busy Writer's Guide*, you'll learn eight techniques that can help you double your word count in a way that's sustainable and doesn't sacrifice the quality of your writing in favor of quantity.

In our new digital era, writers are expected to produce multiple books and short stories a year, and to somehow still find time to build a platform through blogging and social media. We end up burning out or sacrificing time with our family and friends to keep up with what's being asked of us.

How to Write Faster provides you with tools and tips to help you find ways to write better and faster, and still have fun doing it, so that you'll have time left to spend on living life away from your computer. This book was written for writers who believe that there's more to life than just the words on the page, and who want to find a better balance between the work they love and living a full life. The best way to do that is to be more productive in the writing time we have.

Fiction

Frozen: Two Suspenseful Short Stories

Twisted sleepwalking.

A frozen goldfish in a plastic bag.

And a woman afraid she's losing her grip on reality.

"A Purple Elephant" is a suspense short story about grief and betrayal.

In "The Replacements," a prodigal returns home to find that her parents have started a new family, one with no room for her. This disturbing suspense short story is about the lengths to which we'll go to feel like we're wanted, and how we don't always see things the way they really are.

ABOUT THE AUTHOR

Marcy Kennedy is a speculative fiction and suspense writer who believes fantasy is more real than you think. It helps us see life in this world in a new way and gives us a safe place to explore problems that might otherwise be too difficult to face. Alongside her own writing, Marcy works as a freelance editor and teaches classes on craft and social media through W.A.N.A. International.

She's also a proud Canadian and the proud wife of a former U.S. Marine; owns five cats, two birds, and a dog who weighs as much as she does; and plays board games and the flute (not at the same time). Sadly, she's also addicted to coffee and jelly beans.

You can find her blogging at www.marcykennedy.com about writing and about the place where real life meets science fiction, fantasy, and myth. To sign up for her new-release mailing list, please visit her website. Not only will you hear about new releases before anyone else, but you'll also receive exclusive discounts and freebies. Your email address will never be shared, and you can unsubscribe at any time.

Contact Marcy
Email: marcykennedy@gmail.com
Website: www.marcykennedy.com
Twitter: @MarcyKennedy
Facebook: www.facebook.com/MarcyKennedyAuthor